I
DEFEATED
DEPRESSION

A Daughter's Amazing Recovery And Her Father's Loving Response

A Memoir

First Published in Great Britain 2019 by Mirador Publishing

First edition: 2019

A copy of this work is available through the British Library.

ISBN: 978-1-913264-13-0

Mirador Publishing
10 Greenbrook Terrace
Taunton
Somerset
TA1 1UT
UK

I
Defeated
Depression

A Daughter's Amazing Recovery And Her Father's Loving Response

A Memoir

Samantha and Richard Olivier

ACKNOWLEDGEMENTS

A number of people, both professional and personal, have given us invaluable support, advice and assistance through our long journey from first putting pen to paper, or should we say pressing the first key on the laptop, to the moment of publication. To these colleagues, family and friends, we extend our heartfelt thanks:

*David Moore, author of fascinating travel memoir Turning Left Around The World, for his introduction to Mirador Publishing.

*Sarah Luddington at Mirador, the first publisher to do more than say nice things in their rejection email! Thanks for your patience, and for metaphorically holding our hands as first-time published authors through the minefield of manuscript development.

*Nick Presley, former Group Creative Director at Initials and previously a colleague and friend at Triangle, for lending support and creative inspiration that helped to lead us to the final title and front cover design.

*Chris Perowne, Head of Design at Initials, a highly talented designer who somehow managed to find time in his manic weekly work schedules to create and develop several versions of the title and front cover, and for delivering the final version ready for printing.

*Dominic Smales, CEO of 'digital-first' influencers management company Gleam Futures, for advice on how to approach people in the publishing world.

*Anne Steiner, an experienced teacher and friend, formerly a Head of English who diligently read the manuscript and made a number of significant improvements to the text and the layout.

*And finally, Jane (her nom de plume in the book, who is also an experienced Special Needs teacher) whose calm, sensible advice and comments throughout have helped us both keep our feet on the ground whilst constantly striving for the honest truth. You were our port in the storm of reliving our long journey from despair to delight.

Contents

SAMMIE'S CONTENTS

PART 1

Sammie's Foreword

EACH AND EVERY ONE OF us has a journey, many parts of which we have control over and many parts of which control us. This is the true story of my and my family's journey through my clinical depression and suicide attempts.

The point of this story is to let sufferers know that what they are feeling and experiencing isn't forever and that it is possible to lead a happy and fulfilling life. If you have suffered from depression or know someone who has, you will read things in this book that you will be able to relate to, not only on the surface, but within your soul. That is where depression resides after all, and where the healing happens. For sufferers, it is an amateur self-help book. For families of sufferers, it is partly an educational book, and for the curious it will satisfy your need to know the ins and outs of depression and the relationship the sufferer has with suicide. But the good news is that I finally defeated depression and am now leading a happy and fulfilled life despite all the setbacks along my long road to recovery.

What makes our story different is that my father also wrote, chapter by chapter, my family's response to the events as they unfolded. His story may help parents of children who are in the same situation that I was.

I dedicate this book to the millions of people who were not as fortunate as me in seeing a way out, and also to my mum who passed away on Christmas Eve 2012 of lifestyle-related causes. By a message I received from the other side, I believe she was the one who suggested I write this book.

SAMMIE'S JOURNEY

C h a p t e r   1

In which Sammie is introduced to a strange man.

MUMMY THINKS I AM ASLEEP upstairs but I'm actually hanging over the side of the wooden banister trying not to be noticed by the strange man engaged in conversation with her while they both eat dinner.

This was the early stage of what was to be their 38-year relationship. This would be the same banister that I would later slide down from the top to the bottom but fall off halfway down, landing abruptly in a heap on the cold tiled floor of the family home.

At 3 years old I don't have any memories of my parents being together or indeed when Dad married my step-mother. My earliest memories begin 2 years later when Mummy married the man I was inquisitively staring at from the top of the stairs. I'm sure my sister Eve, who was 7 when my parents divorced, does have some recollection.

David is 8 years older than Mummy and lives 180 miles north of our family home in leafy Buckinghamshire. He has his own electrical business and dry-cleaning shop 20 miles south of Manchester. He also has two sons who are several years older than my sister and me. They are from his first marriage which ended suddenly when their mother unexpectedly passed away from a heart attack while getting dressed in the bedroom. Mummy feels it will be for the best if we all move to live with David and his youngest son in the north of the country.

I am fortunate that Dad is in a position to pay for private education for Eve and me, so we are enrolled in a school about 30 minutes away from our new home. I am excited to wear my tunic, shirt, tie, blazer and hat and start my first day. But at the end of the first week I am left wondering why Mummy never gets out of the car to meet us at the school gate with the other parents. I'm getting used to the 5-minute walk up the road along the line of parked cars. Mummy always parks right at the back of the line and I don't understand why.

It takes some adjusting for us all to live happily under the same roof. David and his youngest son have their world turned upside down yet again, with three females moving into their space! David's younger son Charles pretty much keeps himself to himself by playing his guitar hour after hour in his bedroom.

It's the night before Christmas and Eve and I are excited to have Mum's half-brother Liam stay with us over the festive season. I spend hours waiting at the window. His arrival is a clear indication that Father Christmas is on his way. It also means that Mummy is likely to smoke and drink more than usual and unfortunately there are consequences with this. On Christmas Day, Eve and I make eye contact several times across the table and although it is for no more than 2 seconds there is a telepathic exchange of discomfort that is mutual between us. Mummy was just 4 feet 11 inches tall and weighed no more than 140lbs, so by the third glass of white wine it was apparent that the alcohol had begun to take effect. Inappropriate comments and laughter were an inevitable part of the hours spent drinking, and much like any dependency it became more and more frequent. I am beginning to notice that I am starting to actively avoid spending long periods of time in her presence, particularly after 6pm, this seeming to be the crucial point when she goes from being bearable to unbearable to be around.

As I approach my teenage years I'm tending to spend more and more time out of the house on sleepovers at friends but for some reason they aren't being reciprocated. I'm often embarrassed when Mum says something she shouldn't say or something inappropriate, or behaves in such a way that everyone present feels awkward. This is also when she likes to speak badly of my Dad.

I'm old enough to realise that no matter the circumstances of the break-up you shouldn't encourage animosity towards the other parent. Because of this I hold Dad in an even higher regard. He is also the one who later on will drive 4 hours here and back to watch me swim one race in the swimming gala or drive 6 hours to arrange a private meeting with the head teacher to discuss my future. As the months go by, I find I am liking my step-mum Jane more and more. I'm a bit confused though because although I really like her, she's not my real mum and so I feel guilty about how much I like her and about how much I enjoy the regular visits with her and Dad.

Mum, however, will allow Eve to walk the mile home from the train station after school whatever the weather. Sometimes David would pick her up if he was home from work in time. I feel guilty for having these thoughts and I know now that Mum did the best that she was capable of.

The transition from Junior to Senior school is not easy. I'm very athletic but falling behind in academics. Thankfully the Senior school which I now attend is very sports focused and there is a lot of opportunity for me to flourish. It just so happens that it was previously a boys' only boarding school but I am one of three girls to attend that year. It's not like the schools that my friends from the village attend. We get on the bus together but they are dressed in whatever they like, whereas I am dressed in a tunic, shirt, tie, blazer and hat. They all get off the bus at the same stop and I am the only one staying on until the next stop. Some days are better than others. There is no set pattern with the bullying, it can be every day for a week or nothing for 2 or 3 days. It's mainly centered on my uniform with charming comments such as 'posh cow', or 'you think you're better than us'. I know I am privileged to have private fee-paying education but I'm starting to wish I could attend the state-run school with my friends from the village. But I'm enjoying school, making new friends and spending endless hours playing basketball with the boys at lunch time.

As the months go by, more girls attend the school. Some start as day pupils and some as boarders. Amongst the girls you could begin to see groups forming, the boarders and the day pupils being increasingly separated during lesson time as well as lunch periods. I'm not really enjoying my lessons and there are some subjects I dread. I even lose sleep the night before, worrying about being singled out in class to answer a question I have absolutely no idea about.

But the thing I really love is sports. Athletics, swimming, rounders, soccer, basketball, I was really good at anything and everything, so everyone wanted me on their team. I was a keen swimmer and would regularly take part in national competitions. Dad would make the 360-mile round trip in the middle of his work day just to watch me swim one race. I found the anticipation of his arrival to be quite overwhelming.

The swimming teacher was a middle-aged single guy and for whatever reason he seemed to take a liking to me. He would offer to drive me home after a swimming competition and I remember him and Mum talking for hours in the kitchen. By this time David was asleep in front of the TV in the living room. One morning the swimming teacher, Mr. Churchill, stayed over at our house and inevitably he took me to school the following morning. That was very strange and made me feel quite uncomfortable.

Chapter 2

Coming out, America, college and a return to the south.

AT AGE 15, THE PRESSURE was on for GCSE exams. My peers and I were entering a crucial time in our academic lives. I felt overwhelmed much of the time by what was at stake if I were to fail. I remember thinking if I could take a test in the 50 metres freestyle I would have aced it!

To counteract the pressure of academics I threw myself more and more into sports. Lunch times, after school, any opportunity I had to run or swim, I took it. My peers at my senior school were forming romantic relationships and so when I was invited out by one of the boys I felt relieved and jumped at the chance to be following the norm. The boys found my achievements in sports attractive and I was not short of offers when it came to dating. I remember going to the cinema, sitting in the back row with Dean getting closer and closer. But it felt like the worst feeling in the world to me. I likened it to walking on to a stage in a crowd of a thousand people and suddenly realising your skirt is accidently tucked into your knickers! It was simply that physically all-consuming discomfort that you just need to end at the soonest possible moment. I put it down to Dean not being right for me. Needless to say, that relationship didn't go any further. Neither did the next one, or the one after that or the one after that one.

My peers picked up on something that even I didn't know about myself. This was when my life took a dramatic turn for the worse. The months of taunting, bullying and threats began again. It started with a couple of girls, but soon turned into a mass epidemic of most of the kids and even some of the teachers. Breaks and lunch times were spent on my own trying not to make eye contact with anyone who walked past as that would inevitably trigger a comment. This behaviour lasted for months and gathered momentum as time went on.

One lunch time I went into the local town, on my own of course. This was usual for me now as it was my only means of escaping the bullying. On my way back to school I saw two of my favourite teachers walking towards me. They took me arm in arm and said they had come to escort me back to school because there was a group of girls looking for me to beat me up. I was taken into the headmaster's office. He sat me down and told me that for my own safety he was sending me home. Mum came to collect me and we drove back to the village where we lived 20 minutes away.

A few days later and still not understanding the real situation, I told Mum that I wanted to go back to the school to collect my books from my locker as I needed them to revise for my GCSE exams which were starting in a couple of weeks. We arranged with the school for me to return when there would be no one there. As I opened my locker, torn and ripped books fell into a heap on the floor with the screwed-up papers. I salvaged what I could, which wasn't very much, and Mum and I returned home before any of the kids noticed we were there. It was apparent that somehow, they had got access to my locker and pretty much destroyed everything in it.

The school had informed Mum that they would allow me to return to school only to attend my GCSE exams as there would be a tutor present at all times, and Mum would need to come and collect me straight after the exams. The result of all this bullying was that I did not do well in my GCSEs. I knew that if I was to get anywhere in life I needed to gain more qualifications and so I applied and was accepted into Stockport College where I did a National Diploma in Sport Science and then a National Diploma in Leisure Studies.

I was dating a boy called Robert who lived in the same village as me. We were good friends before we decided to take it further. We had a similar upbringing and so we were able to talk to each other about things like skiing holidays without the risk of being ridiculed. He was such a nice boy and I was determined to love him. But no matter how much effort I put into the relationship, I was not able to fall in love with him. I was, however, experiencing feelings towards one of my college classmates. Her name was Joanna. I liked being in her company, I liked to make her laugh and I wanted to spend more time with her. I hadn't given up on Robert and I was still battling with my heart, desperate for him to make me feel like Joanna did. My feelings for Joanna were not totally clear to me, I think because I refused to allow them to surface. I constantly suppressed them. My relationship with Robert ended mutually, and we decided we were better as friends. Needless to say, I was hugely relieved.

At the age of 18 I applied to be a counsellor with the Camp America organisation. My sister had been to upstate New York the previous year and loved it, and so this year we decided to go together. It was such an adventure, and of course it was the first time I was going to be away from home for any great length of time. Everything was new and different, there wasn't much of a settling-in period, it was pretty much straight to work.

The American staff arrived over a couple of days. It was a mixed camp so there were both male and female counsellors and campers. There was one particular counsellor, Karen. She conjured up the same feelings I had for Joanna but this time they were more intense. Perhaps it was because I was so far away from home, but my heart would race, I would get nervous in her presence and I just wanted to be with her. At the same time, I still refused to fully acknowledge my feelings and I can only describe my day-to-day existence as clouded. I was operating in my subconscious because I refused to bring these feelings into the real world. Because of this I felt in a sort of screen saver mode, I wasn't able to clearly see what it was. It felt strange, it felt different, but I didn't know why. It wasn't until later that I found out that the other staff on the camp could clearly see what it was and the rumours had started.

I think Karen was perhaps in a confused state also. She would give me clear signs, then immediately retract them. This fed into my belief that what I was experiencing wasn't right and so I had to continue to suppress these terrifying feelings. Six weeks later I returned from America with a broken heart. I cried a lot from the space that was in my heart created by being such a distance from Karen. Mum caught me crying in my room and asked me what the matter was. I told her I had fallen in love. She hugged me and asked me who my first love was. There was a long pause before I said, "His name is Craig and he lives in America." That was the first opportunity I had to 'come out', but I wasn't ready to acknowledge it myself, let alone share it with anyone, especially my mother.

The months went by and I expected my feelings to subside, but they didn't. So I ended up making a return trip the following year to the same camp in the hope that I would see Karen again. She didn't attend that particular camp that year and I was left with the months of anticipation that had been building inside me and then the bitter disappointment of not being able to see her. I think that my brain just couldn't cope with the years of suppression of my true sexuality, then when I was finally ready to accept it, Karen wasn't there. This was the first time I experienced a panic attack. I would hyperventilate, collapse on the floor and my heart would be racing and my legs were like jelly. I was taken to the camp infirmary where I spent several days before they decided the best thing for me was to go back to England early. I remember thinking one day that my head felt so busy and was constantly preoccupied. It was like a wheel that never ever stops spinning. So many thoughts would enter my mind, most of which I didn't want. It was exhausting to be living constantly in a heightened emotional state.

But I was so relieved to be back in England and at home. Despite this, the panic attacks continued and were getting more frequent and intense. It was like my mind only had the ability to focus on my body. Nothing else could get through. That only exacerbated the panic as every twitch and every heartbeat was magnified so that I had no choice other than to focus solely on my body. Sometimes these attacks would last for 2 or 3 minutes and sometimes they could go on for an hour or more.

As I now know, depression and anxiety are the very best of friends, so it wasn't long before I would become a victim of entrapment within the evil clutches of the repetitive cycle of both anxiety AND depression. My mood and well-being were steadily declining. My mind could no longer cope with the years of suppressed feelings and I could no longer cope with the depression and anxiety. I needed to end these feelings.

I remember the day so vividly. I had a box of painkillers in my room. I took one, then another, then a third and a fourth and finally gave in to my need to survive having taken a total of seven pills. Then of course I became frightened at what I had just done. I didn't know if I was going to wake up the next morning and just be sick, or if there would be any effects at all. I guess most people in that situation would have told their mum, but I just didn't have the nerve to do that. So I ran down to the nearest phone box and called my dad and step-mum Jane in a panic and explained to them what I had done. They told me to go back home, tell Mum what I had done and go to bed. Jane then made a phone call to my doctor's office who advised her that if I had only taken seven tablets I should be fine but I might be a little sick. That's exactly what happened. There were no lasting effects physically apart from the vomiting and I managed to go to sleep.

I woke up the next morning understanding the full extent of what I had tried to do. I knew then that I needed help to cope with the realisation that I was a lesbian, particularly in the sort of community I was living in. It seemed to me that at that moment, my future was pretty bleak. This was a significant event and I was going to have to finally accept these feelings I was having for other women. The first person I told was my mum, and she didn't seem surprised. Slowly I began to tell other family members and then friends. I had mixed reactions. People cried, some hugged me, some said they could no longer be my friend. I had given into it and there was nothing I could do to stop it.

I was at last ready to embrace it and frankly, to shout it from the rooftops. Shortly afterwards I found a group in Manchester called Lesbian Link, and this was to be my first experience of being around like-minded people. I was given an address of the meeting place of the group and so off I went. I had passed my driving test and Mum had allowed me to borrow her car but we weren't to tell my step-dad just yet. I entered a dark high-rise building and took the three or so flights of stairs until I found the number on the door I had been given. There was no sign on the door, just a number. I was to call the telephone number I was given and let them know I was outside the door. I was asked if anyone had seen me come into the building or if anyone had followed me. That in itself was pretty alarming, but in hindsight was a reflection of society's attitudes in those days.

As I entered the room it was like a light switch had been turned on in my brain. I didn't know where to look. There were about thirty girls and women, some playing pool, some dancing, others just chatting. I was introduced to a couple of girls and we immediately got talking. I returned to the club a couple more times before I met Delia. She was to be my first. I remember standing in the gay village in Manchester about to get back in the car to go home and we kissed. It was like a firework display going off in my whole body. This was it, this is what everyone talks about. This is why my friends talk so much about their boyfriends, it's because they make them feel like how I had just felt.

We dated for just a few months and although it wasn't a particularly healthy relationship it was the beginning of my journey and acceptance of myself as being gay. I have never been one for using the words lesbian, dyke or homo, but back then this is what we were all called. To this day I still cringe at the use of those words. I much prefer the term gay, which to my mind is short, non-offensive and gentler on the tongue.

Growing up in a small village was going to be difficult if I was to indulge in my new, accepted self. I began to think about moving to where my dad and step-mum lived. My sister was already there as she had left a few years earlier, but I was worried how Mum would cope if we both left her. I decided to stay for a while and finish my college course. I started to talk to my close friends about my sexuality. You could tell they were desperately trying to react in a positive, non-judgmental way but it was clear there was an element of discomfort and awkwardness and so to dilute this I would always follow by saying 'I'm sorry!' And I genuinely was sorry for altering the dynamics of our friendships. However, the standard response from most of my so-called friends was 'you don't fancy me, do you?' That was certainly the clear concern that my so-called friends in our village had.

Once I finished college I decided I needed to change the path of my journey and so I made the move to the south of the country. I knew it would be difficult to leave Mum. I felt that Eve and I were leaving partly because, to be absolutely frank, most evenings it was almost unbearable to be around her. My only means of escape was to go to bed. I soon got into a routine of going to bed at around 8.30 or 9 o'clock to escape the usual routine.

When I finally told my best friend in the village, she promptly decided I was no longer worthy of her friendship and so this added to the justification for the move. I just felt that I was ready for a new start. I had grown to love my step-mum, and I felt that I would just be much happier living with her and Dad.

So I packed up all my belongings, said goodbye to mum and David, and moved to Buckinghamshire to live with Dad, Jane and my step-brother Daniel. I wanted to continue studying in order to catch up with some of my lost education, so I enrolled in Buckinghamshire University in High Wycombe. It was a 2-year Higher National Diploma in Leisure Studies. Here I met other gay people, both male and female, but I still also encountered some negativity. That didn't get in the way of me having relationships but there were times when I was still anxious and confused. Looking back on it now, I realise that admitting and then coming to terms with one's different sexuality is one of the hardest and certainly most significant moments in anyone's life. Perhaps if society had been more enlightened than it has become now it would have been easier. But at the end of my teenage years I was able to accept the situation and start to think about my future life.

Chapter 3

Barbara, the private clinic, BPD.

LIVING WITH DAD AND JANE allowed me to explore my sexuality while also living in a calmer, more accepting and loving place. I felt safe experiencing new friendships, so the following years were spent experimenting with roles and relationships.

I secured various jobs in the media industry including the music TV channel *VH1*, but it was a love/hate relationship. The thrill of seeing the television commercial you had filmed the previous week or the interview with Paul McCartney where I was three feet behind him, added a whole new dimension to my life. However, the hate element of the industry was the attitude of the egotistical producers and directors to whom I reported, because they clearly relished the power trip their position somehow condoned. The high point of my media career was without doubt my participation in an interview with the British rock band *Genesis*. After the departure of the iconic Phil Collins, Ray Wilson stepped in to take over as the lead singer. Calling All Stations was his debut album and *VH1* were to interview all members of the band. Being a *Genesis* fan as a result of my dad constantly playing their records, I approached the producer and asked if I could volunteer for the day. The interview was held in a social club in Surrey near where the band lived. When the crew and I arrived, they were already set up and practising. Each one of the band members was interviewed for approximately 10 minutes in a room off the main area. As a keen drummer myself I was instantly drawn to the sessions drummer who was being used for the day, and he talked me through the massive drum kit. Imagine my surprise when he asked me if I would like to take a seat on the throne (which is what drummers call their special seat), and play along while Mike Rutherford, Tony Banks and Daryl

Stuermer played their own parts. I had access to about twenty individual drums but only had the courage to use about four which was what was required in order to keep the beat going! This was one of the highlights of my media career and an occasion that I will never forget.

I got invited out by my work colleagues but I never accepted their invitations. I always felt so different to everyone else there. The girls were talking about the boys they fancied and the boys were talking about their conquests with the girls. I didn't dress like the other girls and I didn't have the confidence to contribute to any of the conversations and inevitably after so many times of me not accepting their invitations, I was no longer asked to join them on a night out.

Then came a momentous development in my life. I was still living with Dad and Jane when I met Barbara. She was in the local pub across the road from our house. The *Full Moon* was one of the few places where I felt quite comfortable. It had an easy and relaxed village pub atmosphere, not like the London bars and clubs my peers were frequenting. I was often put in the position where I had to make a rapid decision about whether to 'come out' or not. "Do you have a boyfriend?" is a common question you are asked in your 20's!

Barbara was 12 years older than I was and she was already successful in her job selling software for an information technology company in Hemel Hempstead. She also had her own house in a village just 15 minutes away. Our relationship blossomed into full-blown love and 6 months later I moved into her one-bedroom home which backed onto the Grand Union Canal, with the added bonus of having its own mooring rights. By now, I was also working in a sales support role for a small IT company. I was doing well and was always going above and beyond what was expected of me. I would often arrive early and leave late in order to achieve more than my daily goals. I was the only female in the office but that suited me fine as I seemed to be able to get on better with the guys than the girls.

In November 2004, I went to the local supermarket to get my usual lunch time sandwich and bag of crisps. I used to take the same route there and the same route back every day. I like familiarity and routine and so I relish every opportunity for yesterday to be like today and today to be like tomorrow. As I was approaching the building where the office was, I was very suddenly overcome with an immense fear of returning to my desk. I didn't know why this was happening but I did know that I did not have a choice other than to not return to my office that day. Instead, I walked the short distance to my car and called my boss to explain that I wasn't feeling well and that I was going straight home. The feelings of fear, confusion and unfamiliarity were so intense that they made me physically unwell. For the next 2 weeks I remained in bed, paralysed by the fear and worry of everything. I felt like my brain had blown. I could almost feel a physical change in my brain. I was crippled by panic attacks, anxiety and full-blown depression to the point where it was clear that I needed some medical intervention if I was to get out of this.

My parents took me to a psychiatrist and at long last I was able to say the words out loud, "I don't want to live anymore." These were the same words I had been suppressing and unwilling to acknowledge for many years. As soon as a medical professional hears those words there are procedures that are put in place. I was immediately put on medication and referred to a private clinic in outer London where they specialised in treating people with addictions, anxiety and depression. The clinic was in Harrow-on-the-Hill, a short distance from Harrow School, one of the UK's most distinguished and expensive private boarding schools. Their most famous pupil was none other than Winston Churchill.

Barbara was still working and taking care of the home, as well as trying to understand what was going on and why I needed to stay in the clinic. I remember sitting in the dining room on the first day with the other patients. Dad and Jane were with me for lunch but were soon having to leave me. I recall the tears streaming down my face, and I could see how distressed Dad and Jane were getting too. But I had no choice, I had to go there because if I didn't I would not have survived another day in the outside world.

I was given my own room but it was monitored frequently and there were several holes in the walls where the hooks used to be. I was encouraged to attend all the available therapy sessions. Some were group focused and others were on a one to one basis. Counselling, psychotherapy, and psychiatry became the norm for me. I would meet with my psychiatrist frequently. Sitting on his couch I would beg him to help me and plead with him to save my life. You could see in his eyes he was trying so hard and maybe even feeling a little of my pain.

Daily intensive therapy was prescribed along with anti-depressants and anti-anxiety medications. The combination of drugs and my new intolerably painful existence of wanting to end my life but being too terrified to go through with it, made me unrecognisable, not only to others, but also to myself. It felt that suicide would be my new best friend. That word came up a lot in the next few years. Suicide had a relationship with me and I had a relationship with suicide. We almost became like best friends, but it was a very one-sided relationship because it wouldn't allow me to have other friends or family in my life. It wanted me all to itself and not to share me with anyone or anything else. Whenever I had the opportunity, I would fight to let the outside world in, but suicide got angry and pushed those comforting and familiar feelings away. Suicide was jealous of anyone else who was in my life and constantly fought to be my one and only friend.

I met a girl in the clinic named Leona. Once we had both got to the point where we could make conversation with each other, we became friends. She was in because she had bulimia. At meal times she was always supervised, sometimes it took her hours to eat just a small amount and then she had to be watched for hours afterwards to make sure she didn't throw up what she had just eaten. Leona and I became buddies. She was a smoker but I wasn't. I had been in the past but I had managed to kick the habit. I hung out in the smoking room occasionally as I liked the way it smelled. People would ask why I would be in there but never smoke and my reply was always the same, "Because I don't want to die a smoker." I was so sure I was going to die that it was a case of when and not if, and so when people found out I had died they wouldn't say 'well, she was a smoker', as if that one nasty habit is the only cause of one's death no matter what the circumstances.

Leona and I started hanging out more often. On one occasion in between my 30-minute safety check we ran out of the clinic to the nearest shop and bought a bottle of vodka. We were surrounded by about a dozen or so boys in their tail suits as they were from Harrow boys' school just up the street. We felt like fugitives on the run. We got back to the clinic just in time before anyone noticed we were gone and stashed the vodka. That evening we met up again and started to drink the bottle. But our conscience got the better of us as we were surrounded by people who were needing in-patient care because of their alcoholism. We decided that it was a bad idea and so we ditched the bottle outside of the grounds.

My family would write to me and visit me in the clinic, but it was like seeing a silhouette, thinking there is someone there but I couldn't be totally sure. I was losing the physical and emotional connection with reality and the outside world. This was to be accelerated by a piece of mail that arrived for me one day. Mum had sent me a card. On the front was a happy smiley face. I opened it up only to be traumatised by the words inside, 'now you know how I feel'. To be honest I was in disbelief, but it also gave me validation that what I was experiencing was real. It made me angry but I was at long last able to blame someone for my situation. Later that day during my appointment with my Psych I walked into his office and dropped the card onto his desk from a height and yelled out, "Is it any fucking wonder I'm round the twist?" The look of shock and concern covered his entire face and of course the hour-long session was dominated by this event.

I remember my sister telling me how nice it was outside; the sun was out and the sky was blue. I wasn't able to process what that meant. I had lost the ability to feel. I would hear the conversation but I had lost the ability to listen. The sun was shining but I couldn't feel that it was. My sister brought her newborn daughter into the clinic in the hope that it would make me happy. Suicide only allowed my eyes to see this joyful, happy, innocent child. I was not allowed to have any feelings that went with seeing her and becoming an auntie for the first time.

I was desperate to feel anything, so I would frequently hold my hand underneath the hot water dispenser on the drinks machine, but it had no effect. It would burn but I didn't feel it and so I kept doing it. Bandages were put on the burns so there were no lasting effects and the drinks machine was put 'out of order'. The relationship I had with suicide intensified to the point where I once climbed up a tree and stood on a branch with a scarf tied around my neck. I stood on that same branch for several hours over the next few weeks doing exactly the same thing, wondering if that day would be the day that the branch would snap. But no matter how hard I tried and how determined I was, the branch never did give way.

I tied the telephone cable from my room around the light fixture in the bathroom but I was caught by a staff member standing on the toilet. That incident led to me being moved to what the residents called the Hannibal Lecter suite! It was floor to ceiling glass and was situated by the nurses' station. I didn't care though because I had no feelings. Nothing but emptiness.

When I hear people say suicide is the coward's way out, I have to admit it infuriates me. From the second we are born we are made and taught to survive, it is human nature to survive. Taking that step off the tree branch or in front of the train goes against human nature, which makes it the bravest thing you could ever do. But if suicide was easy I would not be writing this book now. When my psychiatrist was informed that I had missed our appointment because I was up the tree with the scarf around my neck, he made the decision to section me under the UK's Mental Health Act.

For the first time in months, I actually felt something. My psychiatrist saying out loud in the reception area of the clinic, "Samantha Olivier, I am sectioning you under the Mental Health Act under section 5:2. You are no longer free to leave this facility and will be detained for a period of 48 hours." I was horrified. I had lost my freedom, lost my ability to try to end my life. I had missed my chance.

By now I was getting used to having a nurse by my side 24 hours a day. I had to sleep with my door open and the nurse sitting in my room all night, making sure I wasn't going to harm myself. Section 5:2 stated that I had to be assessed by two outside specialists to determine if the section would be upgraded to a permanent detention. I had to convince them that I had made a mistake in wanting to end my life and that it would never happen again. To be brutally honest, I felt that the only mistake I had made was that I got caught and was sectioned. But I actually passed the assessment and the section was lifted. I guess that they must have seen many poor people who were in a much worse state than I was, although at the time I could not possibly imagine that.

It was not long before my psychiatrist suggested that I try a weekend home visit to see if I would latch onto that happy reality. I was terrified. I had gotten used to not having to deal with anything other than what was going on inside my mind. I didn't have to pay bills, open mail, go to work, drive, follow the news, cook, clean or do laundry. Frankly, I had forgotten that in my absence, Barbara was having to do all that. So I agreed to the weekend visit, but as it turned out I wasn't ready.

Suicide and me were still best friends and I still felt I could never shake it off. The first night I was home, I got into my car and drove up the M40 to Birmingham. I pulled into a service station and took all the medication I had with me. I sat in the car for hours trying to end my life with an overdose. But then I panicked. I called my psychiatrist and asked him for help. I wanted to take the pills but I didn't want to take the pills. It was a Saturday night and he was out to dinner with his wife and some friends. He told me to sit tight and that he was coming to get me. A couple of hours later he arrived and I got into his car. He drove me straight back to the clinic. We were in silence for most of the journey. I didn't need to talk as I had so much going on inside my head. Travelling at 70mph down the motorway was an opportunity for me to throw myself out of the car but of course I never did.

I was back in the clinic and back in my place of safety. For the next few weeks I continued with intensive cognitive behavioural therapy as well as the medication. I have always been compliant in taking my medication. After more sessions with my psychiatrist I was then diagnosed with something called Borderline Personality Disorder. I didn't understand what it meant, but learned later about the extremes of emotions it can create, and this is something I know I have to live with. As Dad and Jane often tell me, I am all about one hundred percent. One hundred percent up or one hundred percent down. But honestly, I will take any medication now to help make me feel well again.

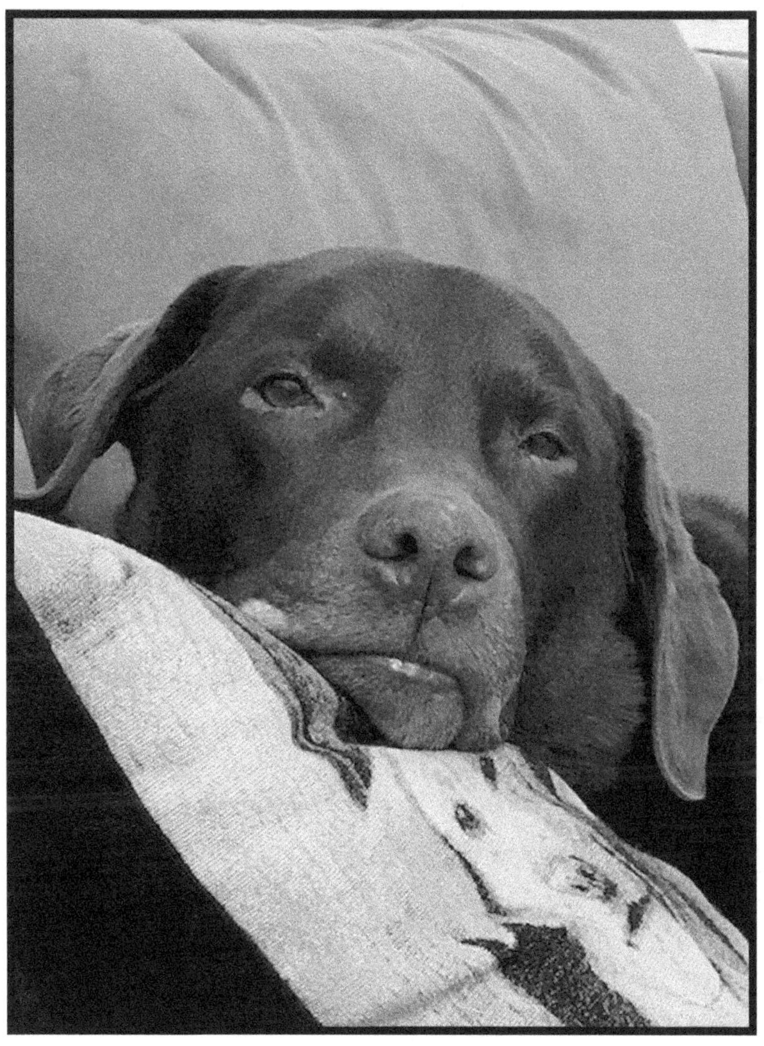

My very best friend, my Hugo

Chapter 4

The spectre in the wood, more therapy, my new job, Hugo and Pets Alone.

DOCTORS AND THERAPISTS THOUGHT THEY were perhaps seeing an improvement in my mood and they tried again at a weekend home visit.

Dad and Jane were in the process of moving house. They had purchased an old barn in the Chiltern Hills and having it renovated to make it their dream home. In the meantime, they were renting a holiday home on a long-term let while they were waiting for the barn to be completed. Inevitably the completion date kept being put back. The holiday let was such a lovely, secure place. It was situated at the top of a country lane. There were just a few properties but it was very secluded, surrounded by green fields as far as you could see. One had been rented by none other than *Rick Wakeman*, the virtuoso keyboard player in the progressive rock band *YES*. Dad was excited because he had always loved *Wakeman's* music, both in the band but more especially with his solo albums. So he popped an Xmas Drinks invitation through the door, but was disappointed to receive no reply. I had comfort, safety and security with Dad and Jane but I also had the anxiety of being somewhere unfamiliar. I always thought something bad would happen whenever I went to a new place which is why I avoided them. I lived in constant fear, which fed the anxiety and that in turn fuelled the depression which kept the relationship with suicide going strong.

It was a restless first night at the cottage and I was relieved to see the daylight the following day. As I opened the curtains in my bedroom all I could see were fields and at the end of the field was a wooded area. The next significant event came on very suddenly and without warning. My brain was telling me that if I entered the wood that would lead to my death. It was as clear to me as writing this paragraph. There was absolutely no doubt in my mind that in order to end my life all I had to do was run through the field and into the wood.

I was terrified because what I had fought so long and hard to accomplish was now an easy fix. I was suddenly faced with a way out. All I had to do was run and it would be taken care of. Jane came into my bedroom just at the point when I was facing the decision on whether to run or not. She could see I was distressed, confused and frightened. I was convinced this was real but it was Jane's responsibility to make me see that this was not reality, that it was not happening. I was actually ready to take off in my nightwear across the fields and into the wood.

Jane was able to comfort me in order for me to regain a sense of calm. She did, however, have to close the curtains so there was no visual reference. The perception that death was merely a few easy steps away was based on a visual interpretation of what my brain was telling me was possible. This is why I am a great believer that there is a profound physical alteration in the brain when it sustains long term trauma such as depression.

Having given this significant event a lot of thought, I have come to the conclusion that it was my sub-conscious giving me the opportunity to end my life and making me realise that actually, this was not what I wanted. All I remember after this one-off delusional episode was laying on the sofa with a blanket over me, exhausted from the short journey my mind and body had just been on. I could see that Dad and Jane were shocked and distressed also. Needless to say, they called the clinic that morning and I was readmitted that day.

I guess for Dad and Jane, nothing had changed. I was still extremely unwell and possibly even more so now that I was seen to be delusional. For me, however, something did change. I had an easy opportunity to end my life or so I thought, and with the help of Dad and Jane I had declined. Somewhere in the trauma of it all I made the decision not to run and not to end my life.

When I returned to the clinic I was actively participating in the group therapy sessions. The art class was my least favourite as I am the least artistic person you will ever meet. My talent starts and ends with drawing stick people! The therapist could see I was sitting doing nothing but actually I was comparing the self-harm cuts on the arms of the patients, including my own. There was one guy who had deep scars that resembled a railway track and fresh wounds all the way up both of his arms. I remember thinking that when he gets better, he would find it difficult to wear T-shirts when out in public. The therapist could see I wasn't taking part in the class and so she set me a task.

"Sammie, I would like you to draw your feelings," she said. This was even easier than drawing a stick man. I took a blank sheet of white paper, a black crayon and I started in the middle of the page and drew the darkest circle the crayon would make. I went over it and over it until I was satisfied it wasn't going to get any darker. I then took the same crayon and I shaded the rest of the page, the farther away from the circle the lighter the shading. Then, in the top, right-hand corner of the page I drew a yellow sun with an 'X' through it and an arrow pointing back towards the circle. This represented my current entire life. Most of it was in complete darkness with an occasional glimpse of light but only to be pulled back fully into the darkness again.

After three months of intensive psychotherapy, psychiatry and counselling the money had finally run out. Insurance had covered a small part and Dad had covered the majority. I was still too unwell to be living in the outside world but Dad explained that I had come to the end of the road at the private clinic. I was eventually transferred to the psychiatric ward of a National Health Service hospital close to my home. When Dad and Jane left me in the care of the staff I could see this was extremely difficult for them, probably even more so than leaving me at the clinic. I can well imagine there was a tear shed when they returned to the car.

The atmosphere was disorganised and chaotic, and the range of the mental health issues of the patients was extreme. Unlike the clinic, this hospital did not specialise in certain conditions, they just had to accept anybody and everybody. As I was shown to my room a member of staff checked my bag for alcohol, drugs and sharp objects. My headphones were taken as well as the shoelaces from my trainers. The shared bathroom was right across the hallway from my room which was at the end of the corridor. I lay on my bed for several hours listening to and being terrified by the sounds. Screaming and crying were dominating the area. As the evening drew to an end I quickly ran across the hallway to use the bathroom one last time before going to bed. I wasn't able to sleep because of the constant noise and clear distress of the patients.

There was one sound that stood out and was particularly close to my room. One of the patients was apparently masturbating outside my door. I knew this as a staff member realised what was happening and had a conversation with her about how it was unacceptable and that they had spoken about this before. It was a restless night with little or no sleep. I was waiting most of the night for the next morning so I could ring Dad and ask him to come and get me.

"Dad, I don't belong here, this is not going to help me, please take me home," I cried. I know Dad has always been a good salesman but he did an outstanding job that morning! They must have agreed that it was potentially more harmful for me to stay because by the afternoon I was back home. He then had to attend a meeting with all the mental hospital staff to try and convince them that I could be treated as an out-patient. We awaited the outcome of the meeting with great trepidation, so I was overjoyed when they finally agreed.

For the next two years I drifted from one day to the next. The depression was still there as it was feeding off the anxiety. The anxiety of new places had heightened and an immense fear of flying had also developed. Barbara and I had booked a skiing holiday with some friends and it involved an early start at 3.30am. We loaded the bags and skis into the car and with just minutes to go until we needed to leave for the airport I was completely overcome by fear. I said to Barbara there was no way I could go on holiday. I couldn't explain it at the time, I didn't know what words to use to describe the feelings. I had to explain to Dad and Jane that I had become terrified of flying and so had refused to accompany Barbara on a holiday that I would normally have enjoyed. Needless to say, my bags were off-loaded from the car and Barbara, no doubt feeling anxious and angry at the same time, set off for a skiing vacation with our friends while I remained at home having just intensified the anxiety by giving into it.

THERE WERE FAMILY EVENTS TOO that I couldn't attend because of my anxiety. On one occasion, all our family were about to fly up to Scotland to stay in a small castle that Dad had rented for the weekend, but the day before the same old terror returned and they had to cancel the trip. The fear seemed to be getting worse and I was unable to break it. This seemed to me to be just one more insurmountable hurdle in my life.

I was fortunate to have eventually overcome this by the generosity of my family who all contributed to my attending the British Airways fear of flying course at London's Heathrow Airport. It is a full day commitment with the morning being a lecture by an experienced pilot as well as a flight engineer. The workings and mechanics of the aircraft are explained in detail in order to educate the audience on how an aircraft performs. I must admit this gave me some reassurance that we weren't going to crash every time I flew! After lunch the group, which was about 50 or 60 people, boarded a bus to the main terminal and we were ushered through the restricted areas to the boarding gate where a small commercial aircraft was standing. Four people out of the group were simply too terrified to enter the plane, but the rest of us nervously took our seats. There was a constant narration over the P.A. system from the pilot explaining the different sounds the aircraft was making. Several of the passengers found the experience overwhelming and were reduced to tears purely out of fear. I was fortunate in that I was able to see the benefit that I would get from this experience. The only other option was for me never to fly again for the rest of my life and I was determined not to let this happen. We flew for approximately 30 minutes and then landed back at Heathrow. When the aircraft returned to the stand there was an almighty cheer from the passengers, it being a combination of relief and accomplishment. For most people this was a life-changing experience, and I have to say that I have flown many times since and my fear of flying has disappeared. I am so grateful that I was able to conquer what could have been a huge restriction in my lifestyle.

It has taken me 12 years to find the right words to describe anxiety and panic attacks. I can only describe it as a total body experience. In fact, it's more than a total body experience, it includes your mind as well as your soul. It's also an outer body experience in which the mind and body go through such trauma during the time of a full-blown panic attack that it is completely debilitating. It is the fear of everything, including your own breath.

I needed to get back into work at some point. An old work friend contacted me asking if I would be interested in working with him. It seemed a good opportunity for me to get back into the workplace. He had started his own smart home distribution company and was ready for his first employee. The hours were fairly flexible and I spent a lot of time on my own which was ideal at the time. The office was in an old warehouse in a small business park, the only heating system being a space heater that was typically used in outside areas. I liked working for Colin. I loved the gadgets and technology that surrounded me and I particularly enjoyed doing an occasional installation in a client's home.

Barbara and I were still very much together and soon after the law allowed, we decided to make our relationship official so we had a civil partnership ceremony. It was a small lunchtime occasion with family and close friends. Barbara and I had a room booked in the hotel that night but yet again I was overcome with the thought of sleeping away from my home and although I did make it through the night, it was not what you might call wedding night bliss.

I must admit that Barbara and I were not the best couple at dealing with finances. In fact, we were both pretty irresponsible when it came to paying the bills. We loved cars and gadgets, and just could not resist buying them. I realise now that it was totally irresponsible but we were on this treadmill and couldn't get off. We had to remortgage the house as we had racked up so much debt and had no way of paying it off. A long-time family friend, Dennis Tiller, was our financial adviser and he was able to put things in place so we could start from zero again.

I was still enjoying my job with Colin and it was still flexible to a point but I was also getting more and more responsibility. However, I began to notice that I was getting headaches frequently and at times was struggling to keep myself awake at my desk. I had mentioned the heating system to my step-dad, David who was a heating engineer, so on his next visit down with Mum from Derbyshire he asked me to show him where I worked. He immediately said that I should get to the doctor's surgery and be tested for carbon monoxide poisoning. The test came back positive and I was close to being given oxygen. It was fortunate that I was able to leave the office every day so my body had a break from the fumes. Unfortunately, it meant that the job had come to an end as Colin was unwilling to acknowledge the issue. Even Dad couldn't persuade him to improve the working environment.

Once again I found myself unemployed and fearful of the pressure of getting a job that I would not be able to handle. The 9 to 5 with an hour for lunch routine was just so terrifying to me. A friend of mine, Sasha, had started her own dog walking business. She had three or four regular clients and needed some money and so we agreed a sum of £500 for me to purchase the name 'Pets Alone' and the small client list.

Barbara and I had just bought a lovely chocolate Labrador from a local breeder and we called him Hugo. I was completely in love with this dog and so when I had the opportunity to walk dogs as a job, be my own boss and set my own hours, it was absolutely perfect for me. *Pets Alone* began to grow through word of mouth and by now I had a full working day, sometimes walking as many as eighteen dogs a day, although not all at the same time I hasten to add!. I also made home visits to put down food for cats, so I was kept busy every day, which was good for me.

Barbara had also changed careers and was now working as a police officer for British Transport police. She introduced me to her new friends who were also in the force. I remember one night we were all socialising and they were talking about the well-known phrase, 'if you're in the force you get a divorce', because apparently the divorce rate is quite high for police officers. I was proud of Barbara for getting into the force but I couldn't help notice that she used any opportunity to show her badge. It was the same with her friends. I believe the term to describe it is a power trip. She started to tell me about incidents that she had responded to that day. Being in the transport police meant that she was dealing with an occasional 'one under', which was when someone had jumped to their death in front of a train. The public were always just told that there had been an incident which is why the train had been delayed. I never knew how to respond when she told me she had to walk the track to collect body parts, and I could never decide if I wanted those details or not.

C h a p t e r   5

Bye-bye Barbara, learning to live on my own, DBT, a little light at the end of the tunnel

APRIL 30TH 2010 IS A DATE I will never forget. No matter how hard I try, it is etched onto my brain. Barbara had not returned home from work until the morning as she was working nights. I had gone to work as usual. My business was doing well and no matter what the weather, I was regularly walking about 8 miles a day.

As I returned home I went upstairs to find Barbara. She was on the third floor at the top of the house. We hadn't slept in the same room for several months as I was constantly being woken up by her haphazard working pattern. I sat on the bed and asked her how her work had been. She said to me, "I have something to tell you." I immediately responded with, "Have you met someone else?" and she replied, "Yes." At that very moment, my journey into recovery from clinical depression was severely interrupted. I crumbled in front of her, weak, pathetic and in disbelief.

Our 13-year relationship and 2-year civil partnership had come to an end and I felt that my life had come to an end too. The thought of being on my own was so terrifying I wasn't even able to process it. My brain went at a hundred miles an hour straight back to wanting to end my life.

That night Barbara was in the bathroom. I could hear her on the phone saying, "I miss you too, I've done it, I've told her." I was so full of rage, I used a screwdriver to unlock the bathroom door from the outside, and I grabbed her phone and ran out of the house. I smashed it on the footpath at the side of the house so she could no longer talk to 'Natalie'.

Natalie was apparently an old friend from when they were growing up. They lived in the same area of north London and went to the same synagogue. Thirty years later, they had reconnected through social media and met up for coffee. The relationship had been going on for several weeks. The night shifts Barbara was apparently working were actually nights spent in a hotel with Natalie. The sympathy I had shown for her double shifts and late finishes must have surrounded her in guilt, or maybe she was now so emotionally detached from me and so attached to Natalie that there was no guilt. I really didn't know what to think. Barbara called the police that night after I smashed her phone up. When they arrived, we were told that one of us needed to sleep somewhere else. One copper to another, I didn't stand a chance of being heard. My account of the evening was taken into consideration but I was asked to leave.

The house we lived in was owned by both of us. Barbara point-blank refused to move out. She replaced her phone and carried on in front of me having phone calls with her new girlfriend. This alone completely ripped me apart. The atmosphere was so awful. She wasn't home much and all I could think about was that she was with her. It got too much one evening and so to dilute the pain, I drank a bottle of wine. That of course didn't help and the pain just intensified. The alcohol gave me the courage to digest all the medication I had. I laid on the floor in the kitchen not knowing what would come next. I got frightened and sent a text message to my good friend Tamsin telling her what I had done. Moments later a neighbour who happened to be a police officer came bursting through the front door and saw me sprawled out on the kitchen floor dazed, drunk and incoherent. To be perfectly honest, I don't actually know the course of events over the next few hours. My only recollection was waking up in the hospital the following morning.

Dad and Jane came to collect me from the hospital. I sat in the back of the car and not a single word was said. I was still very much in a daze. The mental suffering didn't ease up at all. I lost my appetite and regularly went for several days without any food at all. When I did eat, for some reason it was salad peppers but that really was all I could digest. I would wake up in the middle of the night literally in shock with tears already streaming down my face. I couldn't bear another waking moment. The days were so long and the nights were interminable too. Sleep was so disrupted I had lost all concept of which was night and which was day. I somehow managed to keep my clients and still found the strength to go to work. Not because I wanted to, but because I needed to fill my days.

We couldn't stay as we were, living in the same house. Something needed to change. With Barbara's refusal to vacate the home I reluctantly found a small two-bedroom terraced cottage in the same town to rent. It was a two up, two down, very small but with a cute back yard. When I woke after the first night I knew this wasn't the place for me. My anxiety levels went through the roof. With the added unfamiliarity of my surroundings this only fed into my already detached reality. Living constantly in a state of wanting to die is like another dimension. The thoughts and feelings are unique to that experience and thank goodness for that.

Somehow, I managed to maintain my dog walking duties, because it was the only thing that was now familiar and gave me comfort. The darkness and disconnection from familiarity deepened and thoughts of suicide were thriving. I sat at the top of the stairs one morning and gathered all the medication I had, that included anti-anxiety, anti-depressants and benzodiazepines.

Hugo was sat next to me as I emptied and swallowed all three bottles. I knew he would be looked after when I had gone but then I had the thought that it wouldn't be me that would be looking after him. That was enough for my mindset to alter. I was now frightened at what I had done. I called my friend Sasha and told her of my action. The next thing I remember was sitting in the dining room vomiting, with the paramedics taking my vitals. As per my previous attempt, I don't have any recollection of the next few hours. When I woke the next morning, I was in a hospital ward with about six other patients. The lady opposite me looked like she was in her 60s. Almost as soon as I had opened my eyes, she said to me, "The last girl who was in that bed tried to take her life as well." I didn't have the will or the ability to respond.

Frequently, people will react to a suicide attempt with 'she doesn't want to die, it's a cry for help'. It's offensive when someone who doesn't know you, doesn't know your life journey, makes an unfounded diagnosis of attention-seeking disorder. For me at least none of the attempts I made on my life were for attention. They were because I no longer wanted to live, but for whatever reason at the crucial moment before I lost consciousness, I made contact with friends whom I knew could save me.

By this time, I was desperate to return to our house that Barbara was living in. I needed the familiarity and the security that it brought. Dad contacted Barbara and asked her if she would move into the cottage so I could move back into the house. She reluctantly agreed and a few days later I was back in my home. My heart was still very much broken as I still was. I was so focused on getting Barbara back into my life, I kept regular contact with her in order to keep communication open. When she was at work I would go to the cottage and clean, do her grocery shopping and ironing. I did that for several weeks, simply trying to win her back. It seemed to be having an effect. We hung out a couple of times together and even went to our usual holiday spot in Cornwall for a week.

She would call Natalie on a daily basis and ask me to be quiet so she didn't know she was away with me. Barbara was clearly keeping us both close enough until she was able to make a decision as to who she wanted to be with. I rather pathetically went along with it for as long as I could until Barbara announced she no longer wanted me in her life and that I should not go to the cottage or call her. My heart started racing again and I knew immediately what was going to follow.

Barbara was in the transport police and so when I said I was going to throw myself in front of a train she felt it necessary to inform the authorities who then temporarily suspended the trains from London to Milton Keynes! I didn't really mean it when I said it. Death under a train was not something I had thought about. Apparently, most people who are suicidal have a preferred method and for whatever reason, mine was death by hanging. I wonder now if this preferred method is your sub-conscious putting an obstacle in the way because why should it really matter how you do it? As long as you get the job done, right?

I was having intensive outpatient treatment from the National Health Service. I saw a counsellor and a psychiatrist. I carried on with the counsellor sessions and in addition, dialectical behaviour therapy (DBT) was introduced. It was a 1-hour session one day a week and I never missed it. It was in a group setting in an outpatient facility, with mindfulness and thinking in the moment being the main focus. I got a lot from those sessions.

Over the next few weeks my thoughts about ending my life became a little less aggressive. I had reached a point where I had thought I didn't have the courage to kill myself so why put myself through even trying. It was still very prominent in my day-to-day living, but the need to end my life was slowly becoming simply a fascination rather than a reality. That's when I turned to the internet for alternative methods, perhaps something I hadn't thought of previously.

There is an organisation in Switzerland where people with terminal physical illness can end their life legally in a safe and comfortable environment. This became my new interest. There was a chatroom on the web site where people who were at different stages in their journey with this humane way of ending their lives could share their stories. I would frequent the chatroom reading many stories of people who were booked to go in 4 weeks, 3 weeks, 2 weeks and next week. I was envious, maybe even jealous. Their illness allowed them to take this path but mine didn't. I dropped that fascination after a few weeks and turned instead to guns. Gun ownership in the UK is not the norm. It is difficult to buy and own a firearm but most of all, people don't feel the need to own one. I did some research to see what type of gun I would need in order to shoot myself in the head. My research showed that in England there would be no possibility of purchasing a gun quickly which had the capability to blow my head off. I got to a stage where I felt like I had been through suicide methods from A to Z. I had accepted that I simply did not have the courage to see it through. I had tried so very hard and for so very long. Apart from my recovery, that is probably the most effort I have put into anything in my life. Oh, except perhaps my 50 metres butterfly races when I was 12 years old too!

With this acceptance, came for the first time, a little calm. I realised that distraction could be a useful tool at times when my mind would wonder. As I got better at these techniques, my relationship with suicide gradually grew more distant, until eventually my divorce from suicide was made final at the end of 2010.

Chapter 6

Learning my new profession, more medical help and diagnosis, a chance meeting that changes my life.

BY THE END OF 2010, I was beginning to feel calmer. I was happy in my work, I had started socialising occasionally and I was really getting to know myself. I was having outpatient sessions at the local mental health clinic. As I was still on medication, I was required to see the practice psychiatrist every 3 months for a medication review. Typically, I would come out of those sessions frustrated more than anything. In the waiting room, there was a radio that was always turned up and tuned to BBC Radio 2, which was a combination of upbeat tunes and thought-provoking discussions, neither of which I was in the mood for. I couldn't find the power button so I could pull the plug from the wall.

It was obvious that to the psych I was just another patient and someone whom he knew nothing about. He would spend the first 2 to 3 minutes reading my file and then he would ask me, 'how are you getting on with the medication? Any problems or side effects?' That would be the same medication I had been on for 5 years. Staff on the Mental Health teams of the National Health Service would come and go. There was no time to get to know the support staff and in any case the rules and regulations wouldn't allow any sort of relationship building. I saw a counsellor once a month for a general session about my mood and well-being, but it was becoming more apparent that there were people more in need of the service than I perhaps was.

My counsellor suggested that I do a test for BPD, which is Borderline Personality Disorder. It's a relatively new classification of a particular mental health condition. Wikipedia describes it as 'a long-term pattern of abnormal behaviour characterised by unstable relationships with other people, unstable sense of self, and unstable emotions'. It was an intensive multiple-choice test that lasted some 4 weeks. I agreed to do the test and the results came back positive, but only just! So now I had been officially diagnosed as having BPD. I was then referred to another outpatient facility in Dunstable for a half day a week, a 6-week course on mindfulness. It was a relatively new course being offered. I accepted the offer and got started straight away. Every Wednesday between 9am and midday I attended the group session with about eight or nine other people. There was a format that was followed and every session focused on one aspect of mindfulness. It was hard to manage both my job and the course, but I informed my clients of the temporary change of schedule and they were all very accommodating. All, that is, except one of them! It was in this group that I learned about being in the moment. That's something that has to be learned but is enormously beneficial. I took full advantage of every session of the course and I found it quite enlightening. At the end of the 6 weeks, the teacher approached me and asked if I would be interested in attending a course in order to become a trainer and lead future sessions. I was overjoyed by this proposal because it was a clear indication that I was becoming mentally stronger. I gave it some real thought but decided in the end that I was still in need of building myself up. I didn't feel I was in a position to help other people yet. That was something that would come later, and was I believe, a contributory factor in my eventual recovery. There's nothing like having to think about somebody else to stop you thinking about yourself all the time!

I HAD SOME REALLY GREAT friends in Leighton Buzzard, most of which I had met courtesy of Hugo and our daily walks. He has always been an amazing part of my life from the moment he came into it. My business was thriving and my clients, both human and animal, were extremely important to me. I had several dogs that I walked 5 days a week and sometimes twice a day.

Holly the lurcher was such a well-behaved dog, she was so easy to care for and you could see she came from a very loving home. I always looked forward to picking her up for her walks with Hugo and me. I was fortunate enough to live close to a Woodland Trust park which sat on 400 acres so there was no shortage of space. It was a very popular spot for people walking their own dogs for fun and for business. We would frequently bump into people we knew. I found that I was much better at remembering the name of the dog rather than the name of the owner, which at times was a little embarrassing to say the least! Dolly, the cocker spaniel, was a puppy when I met her, and she was only allowed outside in the garden as she hadn't had her vaccinations. She used to make me laugh as she would come running to greet me and then trip up over her own legs and slide across the kitchen floor. I was excited when she completed her vaccinations and she was able to join us on the morning walk.

I had got into a nice routine of a 30-minute mid-morning walk that typically included five or six dogs, then an hour-long walk at lunch time again with another five or six, then another 30 to 60-minute walk in the afternoon with still more. I think it must be a bit like being a school teacher. You have the ones that make you laugh with pure joy and you have the ones that make you cry because they won't listen to you. I had a cocker spaniel and a springer spaniel who were new clients. Layla the cocker had the sweetest face I have ever seen in a dog, and Charles the springer was special because he only had one eye. As it turned out, Layla was going to bring me to tears on more than one occasion because she was a runner.

One afternoon I opened the back door to collect Layla and Charles and was greeted by several pools of vomit in the kitchen. I noticed there was a huge box of chocolates on the kitchen table that had been eaten, and when I say huge, I mean enormous! It was one of those boxes that's about the size of a regular board game. It didn't take me long to realise which dog had climbed onto the table and stolen the Christmas gift. Layla was still vomiting, which was a dead giveaway. I immediately called the owner as I knew chocolate was toxic to dogs and in some cases fatal. They asked me to take her to the vet immediately. I grabbed Layla and the empty box and then drove to the vet which thankfully was less than 10 minutes away. Layla was given charcoal to induce vomiting and then put on a drip. She ended up in the vet's overnight and was very lucky to be alive. Looking back, I think that was the most terrifying moment in all my dog walking career.

Having the responsibility of six dogs at a time is enormous. Each one has their own quirks and character, and sometimes they have health issues that need to be taken into consideration also. Whenever I got a new client, I was always a little nervous for the first few walks until I got to know them. I'm also a great believer that dogs need to run, to be free and play. Early socialising is a really important part of having a new dog. Exposure to as many of life's sights and sounds is also key. Good food, their own bed and routine are what makes a happy dog, which in turn makes a happy owner.

Hugo had been to puppy classes when he was very young. Barbara and I exposed him to as much as possible. The trainer where we took Hugo told me that she didn't think his hips were as they should be as his gait was misaligned. So we took Hugo to the vet to get him checked out. They suggested he had x-rays so we could see what was going on. The results showed that Hugo had severe dysplasia in both of his hips. We were referred to a specialist vet about 45 minutes' drive away in the countryside. The specialist recommended a total hip replacement on the left side. The right was bad too but the left was the one that would be causing the most pain and discomfort. Hugo was just 10 months old when he had his operation. The recovery period was 3 months. For the first 6 weeks, he was confined to just one room downstairs. No jumping on furniture, no climbing up steps and allowed outside only to relieve himself. I brought my mattress and duvet down to the living room and lived downstairs with Hugo for those 6 weeks. It was a long and difficult time in his life and in ours but there was no option, it had to be done. But at the end of the recovery period Hugo had learned how to use his new hip and he was doing great, back to his walks and back to loving life.

My Hugo was now having a great time. He would come to work with me constantly and loved his three walks a day with the other dogs. He was so used to meeting new dogs and always made some new friends. Cozie the shiatsu was one of his buddies and lived a few doors away from us. His owner was also a client who came on our walks, sometimes every day. He was a real character. He was incredibly sweet with people and loved nothing more than a snuggle. He enjoyed meeting other dogs too, but only when he was off lead. But if he was on lead and another dog walked past, his personality changed like a switch and he would launch himself at the other dog, very much in attack mode. Strangely, he would then revert to the sweet and loving boy that everyone enjoyed so much.

I had to try to learn not to get too close to the dogs. Clients would come and go, mostly due to a change in circumstances such as new working hours or family moving close by. Everyone wants to avoid paying for a dog walker if they can have the service for free from a family member. Occasionally my services were no longer needed due to the death of the dog. That was hard to deal with but a hazard of the job, and I learned how to cope with those times too, which helped me to keep my emotions under control.

This really was the perfect job for me. Instead of sitting at home all day in front of the TV, I was out in the fresh air walking several miles a day which was good for me physically and which I began to realise was helping me overcome my depression. More importantly, *Pets Alone* was increasingly contributing to my mental health and well-being. The responsibility of looking after other people's pets gave me a role in life, which in turn started to boost my self-esteem.

By now the business was making enough to give me a steady income. I was able to pay the mortgage, run and maintain my van and have enough left over each month to put a bit into a savings account. At long last I began to feel that I was living successfully and independently.

One of my clients was a labradoodle called Maya who lived at the top of the street about a 3-minute walk from my house. I would walk her 5 days a week and sometimes twice a day. Her owner was a lady from America who was working for *Tesco*, and she had moved here to be with her husband who was in the Royal Air Force. She was actually the one client who was not accommodating the change of schedule one day a week while I took the 6-week course. So, in order to meet her needs, I offered to visit Maya first thing in the morning totally free of charge. This was in addition to the two paid daily visits I was making. The owners seemed to be okay with this and accepted my offer. Maya was a very sweet dog but she was a little mischievous at times. While the owners were at work, they would put her in a puppy pen in the living room. It didn't take her long to realise she could jump over the pen and have free run of the house! Shania, the owner, called me one evening with an upset tone in her voice. She said Maya had chewed one of her T-shirts because I hadn't put Maya back in the pen. I explained that when I left she was in her pen as instructed. The next day, the owner called me again and in a stronger tone accused me yet again of not putting Maya in the pen after her walk. It was clear that the dog was somehow escaping her pen sometime after I had left and before the owner had returned. So the next morning I walked Maya in the park, we played with the ball and she had a great time running with the dogs. As usual, I cleaned her up and returned her to her pen. But this time, I pretended to leave the house and hid behind the door so she couldn't see me. I then peeked through the door, quickly grabbed my phone from my pocket and took the perfect picture of her jumping over the pen! I then sent the image to the owner, with a great deal of satisfaction. A couple of days later Shania knocked on my door and apologised for the accusations and aggressive tone she had taken with me. I appreciated the apology but felt it really shouldn't have happened in the first place. She was a regular client as well as a neighbour, and so I let it go and moved on.

I continued to walk Maya on a regular basis as well as socialising with Shania and her husband and with the neighbours on the street. A few days before Christmas I walked up the street to pick up Maya. Shania had let me know that her sister Carolyn was visiting from the United States. I knocked on the door and was greeted by this lady. She certainly caught my eye. I introduced myself and asked her if she would like to join me on the walk. She accepted and off we went to the park. The conversation was light and we talked mostly about where she lived and about her work which sounded interesting. She was visiting from Cleveland in Ohio, where she had lived all of her life. Her mum lived in Cleveland too and her dad was in Virginia, as they had divorced and he had remarried when she was young.

I received a text the next day from Shania asking if her sister could please join me the following day on Maya's walk. The conversation deepened and quite naturally we began to explore each other's relationship status. I found myself relieved to hear that she was single. She was working in a school environment for kids who had autism and learning difficulties, and she was also studying for a Master's Degree in Couples Counselling. I suppose this must have struck a chord with me, and it certainly helped to bring us closer together. I liked talking with Carolyn and I was enjoying her company more and more. We met up another couple of times between Christmas and New Year. I was at a friend's house on New Year's Eve. I wasn't much into New Year's Eve, I think partly it was the staying up until midnight that I found difficult. But this year, I participated in the festivities with a friend who lived 10 minutes away; she was the owner of Layla and Charles. Just after midnight I got a text from Shania inviting me round to her house. She had a couple of friends over and Carolyn had asked if I would come over. I was undecided about going but finally thought it would do me good. The evening was spent dancing to the *Nintendo Wii* system, not something that I was thrilled about but it was fun to be a part of the celebrations.

By this time Hugo had been alone in the house for several hours and I needed to see to him to let him outside and to make sure he was okay. Carolyn asked if she could come with me and of course I agreed. It turned out to be a night of unexpected passion and what was meant to be a 10-

minute visit to see to Hugo turned into a couple of hours. Carolyn was returning back to the States the following day. I got a text in the morning to say she had changed her flight to the day after so we could spend some more time together. I have to say that it was a fun and exciting 48 hours. To be honest, it was something that I hadn't had or felt in a very long time. I needed it and it was good for me.

When Carolyn returned to the States, I missed her very much and she missed me. We would video call every day. With her work schedule and the time difference, sometimes the calls were not until one or two o'clock in the morning, but we would spend hours just talking about anything and everything. Our relationship, although vicariously through a computer screen, intensified. We were both learning more about each other and liking what we were hearing. My relationship with Shania improved too, which was a good thing considering the tension earlier in the year.

The next few months were spent building *Pets Alone* and continuing with my outpatient appointments as well as establishing a relationship with Carolyn. It was clear we both liked each other very much and wanted to explore it further. In April of 2011 I took my first trip to Cleveland, Ohio to meet Carolyn. The excitement and anticipation were immense along with a natural feeling of nervousness. I hadn't been to America since the traumatic episode at Camp America, but at least I was now much more comfortable with flying. Our feelings for each other which had built up over the previous 4 months were really based on a 'virtual' relationship. Apart from the brief moments we had spent together over the Christmas period, all communication had been through a webcam on a computer screen.

Carolyn rented a duplex in a nice neighbourhood just a few miles west of Cleveland. It was a two-bedroom place that she shared with her roommate, Jimmy. I thought he was a rather odd guy. A heavy smoker, a heavy drinker and a daily dose of marijuana made up his diet! I later learned that Jimmy had dated Carolyn for 10 years until one day when the relationship between them ended and she told me they had become just friends. It quickly became apparent that Jimmy needed Carolyn in order to support himself. He was frequently running out of money and asking for loans from friends to support his unhealthy lifestyle. Jimmy worked at the same place as Carolyn which was next door to where they lived. She had got him a job there several years previously. As I mentioned, it was a school environment for kids with autism.

My first visit to see Carolyn was rather a strange one. I knew she had to work while I was staying there but there didn't seem to be any conscious effort on her part to finish work early or even on time. From about 4pm to 8pm I was left to be entertained by Jimmy. There was a restaurant across the street from the house and so we went there most evenings. Jimmy would insist on buying me jaeger bomb shots in between the several beers. I was so conscious of how much alcohol I was consuming and was quite uncomfortable with it. I have never been anything more than a social drinker, which was clearly not the case with Carolyn's roommate.

My days were spent alone while Carolyn was at work. I spent much of the time on the internet and so one day I decided I was going to get a cab to the local shopping mall. That evening, Carolyn didn't come home and I hadn't heard from her. It got to 10.30pm when she finally sent me a text saying she was at her mum's house and had fallen asleep, so she was going to spend the night there and would see me after work the following day.

I found this strange and very hurtful, because I had travelled all that way to see her and I felt I was being treated poorly. There was no showing me around or introducing me to the local sights. Looking back, I can now see that there was something fundamentally wrong with Carolyn's personality. But at that point, I was disappointed because I was also in love and the 'in love' overtakes every other emotion. When I returned to England at the end of the vacation I convinced myself that the trip was perfect. I so wanted it to be and I did a good job of convincing myself it was, although I did tell Dad, Jane and Eve about the way I had been treated. They were not impressed.

Chapter 7

My worst nightmare comes true. I must stay strong.

MONDAY DECEMBER 17TH 2012. I CALLED Mum to see how she was. I usually speak to her twice a week. I don't recall ever having received a call from her. If ever I want to talk to her I am the one to pick up the phone. I have accepted that is her way. It's similar to the 'I love you's' I will say to her but she is unable to say it back and responds with an uncomfortable grunt.

I am a little worried about her as she has told me she has a stomach upset and is not able to keep any food down. I call her on Wednesday the same week to see how she is doing because she sounds different. I call her mid-morning as I have learned not to call her after 6pm in the evening as she is likely to be intoxicated and I can't have a conversation with her that makes me feel good afterwards. Although it's mid-morning, she sounds like she does at 9pm. I can sense something is not right but I don't want to explore the possibility of her having been drinking in the morning and so I naively put it to the back of my mind. I decide later in the day to call David on his mobile and to get his take on how she is doing. He explains that she is not feeling well but is still able to get out of bed and move around. He doesn't seem too concerned.

It always fascinated me how she was unable to call either of her daughters yet she always had the cordless phone in her pocket whenever she was in the house. David had battled through throat cancer and had a laryngectomy, so his talking skills were pretty limited. He was the most amazing man because throat cancer was one of six times he had beaten cancer. On Thursday December 20th I made my daily call to Mum to see how she was feeling. I was shocked to hear it was David who answered the phone. He said Mum had become weaker overnight, was unable to find the strength to get out of bed and when he had asked her to go see the doctor she had refused. She was so stubborn at times. I spoke to Eve immediately after my call with David and she then spoke to him. The next phone call I got was from Eve telling me she was driving up the M1 motorway. David had managed to persuade Mum to agree to have the doctor visit the house and so Eve was hoping to get there in time for the visit.

The doctor requested that Mum be taken to the hospital immediately and with that information I then got in the car and made the 150-mile journey to Macclesfield hospital. Three hours later I arrived. Mum was in a general ward with Eve and David both by her bedside. As I approached her, I had an overwhelming sense of dread. I was totally unfamiliar with the feelings that this emotion brought with it. As I sat next to her I could see that one side of her mouth was drooping. It was clear she had recently suffered a stroke. I, of course, felt some guilt as the last time I spoke to her on the phone the possibility of her having drunk alcohol in the morning was a real fear. The slurred words during the phone call were of course from the stroke. I never thought at the age of 38 I would be taking my own mum to the toilet. She said she needed to go and so Eve and I were the ones to take her. We managed to get her into the wheelchair and to the bathroom at the end of the ward. She was unable to stand or sit. She was skin and bone, and I was both terrified and horrified at what I was seeing. Between Eve and me, we were able to turn it into a nervous comical event but it was clear that we were both in disbelief at what we were having to do. We got Mum back to her bed and shortly after, the doctor arrived to assess her. He started with the usual questions, "Do you smoke, how long for?" and of course she responded with, "Yes, for 50 years." "Do you drink alcohol?" Yes, was the answer to that one also.

With confirmation of the unhealthy lifestyle, there was no need to carry on with further questioning. The doctor simply examined her physically and said that he could feel secondary liver cancer, which meant it was in other areas also. He ordered a scan of her entire body so it would show exactly how extensive the cancer was. There was little we could do from here on and so David, Eve and I left the hospital for the night.

The next morning, the hospital called Eve and requested that we go down to speak to the doctor. When we arrived, he said, "I'm afraid your mum is very sick and will not be leaving the hospital. But you are free to stay with her outside of visiting hours." Of course, one of the first questions you ask is 'how long?' We were told that they couldn't be certain but it was likely to be just days. What I had expected for years was now an awful reality. I guess I wasn't surprised, just terrified at how the next few days were going to go.

Mum was moved to a different ward in the hospital. Eve and I named it 'God's waiting room'. You could see from the patients that there was no going home if you were in this ward. Mum was in the bed at the far end of the ward next to the window. The view was just a brick wall of another part of the hospital. For the next few hours Eve, David and I were sitting by mum's bedside wondering what would happen next. Every hour or so Eve would put water on a cotton bud and gently run it along her lips. She was in and out of consciousness at this stage and had lost the ability to breathe through her nose.

For some relief, I bought a copy of *Hello* magazine from the hospital shop and as I flicked through, I would put it in front of Mum and Eve, and we would laugh at the models' outfits in the hope it would take our minds off the reality of the situation. That evening, David left the hospital to return home and get some sleep. Eve and I decided we were going to stay through the night. It was the first of three nights we were about to spend there. During a state of her being conscious, she was trying to communicate with me that she wanted something from the one drawer storage chest that was next to the bed. She was asking me for the plastic bag that was in the cupboard. When I put it in front of her, she asked me to put it over her head and a tear ran down her face. I apologised and said I was unable to do that. The only option was to just carry on watching her deteriorate and find another image in the magazine that would bring some light humour to what was now the most surreal situation of my life. As we knew there was only one outcome to this position, Eve and I reluctantly found ourselves willing her to take her last breath.

At that stage my knowledge of the dying process was limited and didn't really go beyond a *Google* search. I was grateful for the increased times Mum was not conscious. They were quiet and calm. I was sat on the right side of Mum by her bedside and Eve was on her left. A curtain separated us from the death rattle that I had recognised coming from the lady next to me. Her daughter had come to say goodbye to her. No more than an hour went by and I heard a trolley and the sound of a long zip being closed. The lady had passed away just three feet away from me. I held my head in my hands as I was in complete disbelief at the situation I was in.

Eve and I got very little sleep that night. We didn't leave Mum's bedside other than to use the bathroom and we were both relieved to see the light of the next day. At about 10 o'clock Eve and I changed places with David and his eldest son Charles. We returned to the house to get some much-needed sleep while David and Charles held a vigil by the bedside. At about 4pm we returned to the hospital. Knowing we wouldn't be leaving until the following morning we were better prepared for the night ahead. The hospital nurses kindly told us we were welcome to use the staff kitchen. We certainly didn't need to use it to cook any food as we had both very much lost our appetites, but the occasional cup of hospital tea was a welcome relief. The night of course was long and uncomfortable. We would both be holding Mum's hand either side of the bed and the other hand was free for us to play a word game against each other on our cellphones. Every so often one of the words we played had some comical value and we would both look up and smile. For that micro-second when we were looking at each other our minds were anywhere other than where we actually were, but the relief was short-lived.

Mum would gasp for breath or suddenly wake up. She was getting very restless and was starting to get verbal. At approximately 6 o'clock on Saturday morning Mum was awake and agitated. She was propped up by the pillows and fairly upright in her position. She used her hand to call Eve into her closer and as Eve responded Mum put her hands around her neck and shouted, "Help me, help me." We were both in complete and utter shock at what had just happened and I instinctively pressed the emergency call button. As the nurse came in, Eve managed to find the words to tell her what had just happened. We both then left the ward and went into the visitors' room where we wept and talked it out. It was one of the most terrifying experiences of our lives and it changed everything from then on. We just had to take a break at this point for about 30 minutes but we knew we had to go back in. We agreed that from now on whenever one of us needed a break the other one would go too, so that way we were never alone with Mum.

I have to admit that I was now frightened of my mum, but it was a different kind of fright to the one that we all experience from time to time. It was like the frightened emotion had taken a new twist and become stronger but in a different way. Not only was I frightened of her dying but I found myself also frightened of her. She was so weak and frail and her physical capability was next to none, so what exactly was I frightened of? I guess it was the lasting memories that these last few hours of her life would bring and how they would impact on my future well-being. A parent on their deathbed is a forever lasting memory. Also, I was frightened at how this was playing out for her. It just did not seem like a peaceful and controlled ending. Up until this point, I had always sat next to Mum on the right side of her. I would intermittently hold her hand, but I could no longer be within touching distance of her in case she lashed out again. I moved my chair to the end of the bed and that is where I sat until the very end.

When full daylight was shining through the window Eve and I again returned to the house to get some sleep and as before, we then came back to the hospital for what would be the final night. I was praying it would be a peaceful night and it was. We were at the stage where we wondered if that breath she just took was her last. Eve and I would send text messages to each other across the bed. 'I really thought that was it', and 'I wish she would just go now'.

The next morning, on Christmas Eve Monday December 24th, Mum was due to have her scan. A male nurse entered the ward and shouted, "Tina Oakes, I'm here to take you for your scan." One of the nurses who was caring for Mum looked up at him and shook his head. He turned around and left the ward. Eve and I returned to the house to get some more sleep, and David was with us also. It was nice the three of us being together, as we had been like ships passing in the night, David doing the day shift and Eve and me doing the night shift. David also had his two sons with him at times and Charles, the eldest of the two, was at Mum's bedside.

At 1.45pm Eve received a phone call from the hospital, and I leapt out of bed and into the hallway. Eve remained completely calm and told David and me that Mum had just passed away. Charles had gone to the bathroom at the time. Apparently, people often wait until they are completely alone before they slip away. Shock, disbelief and relief were the emotions that I was experiencing and they felt so disorganised and chaotic. The three of us made the 45-minute journey back to the hospital, knowing it would be for the last time. We went into the visitors' room and one by one we all went to say our goodbyes. Visiting hours were 2pm to 3pm and so the ward was quite busy, not only with families visiting their sick relatives but also with a group of carol singers who were joyfully singing 'Hark the Herald Angels'.

I was the last one to go to see Mum. I had always been terrified of death because of my depression, and it was the stuff my nightmares were made of as a kid. Tom, the nurse who had been looking after Mum, made the walk with me to where she was. Although I was 38 years old, I asked him if I could hold his hand. Of course, he obliged. The curtain was pulled back and in I stepped. Tom went to pull his hand away but I put a tight grip on it. She was grey and still. She had spent so many days being agitated and restless that I felt she was ready to be in a state of calm. As I got closer I kissed my hand and placed it very lightly on her forehead, all the while still holding Tom's hand. As I left the ward the carol singers were still joyfully sharing their festive cheer.

That evening, Eve and I returned to the south. We drove together in her car as we didn't want to be apart. Eve had her family to get back to for Christmas Day and I was anxious to see Dad and Jane and Hugo. When I got home, I packed another bag and Hugo and I spent the night with Dad and Jane at their house.

December 25th is supposedly when the world is a beautiful place and everyone in it is happy, playful and excited. But Christmas 2012 was a haze for us. A combination of trying desperately for a familiar feeling, but being constantly overtaken by my lack of sleep amid highly confused and chaotic emotions. Christmas Day was everything you would imagine it to be when your mother has just passed away.

Chapter 8

A new life beckons. A chance to leave my demons behind.

BECAUSE MUM HAD DIED OVER Christmas, the arrangements were very delayed and we had to wait three weeks before the funeral could take place. This was when I found myself going more and more to the gym. I went obsessively about six times a week. Combined with healthy eating and portion control I lost almost 30lbs in 5 months. In the weeks following her death there were times when I would be on the cross-trainer and suddenly encased by the sorrow of not having my mum any more, and I would have to leave the gym for fear of not being able to control my emotions. Occasionally I would go back the same day and try to complete my workout.

Moments of deep sorrow and the inability to believe that my mum had died lasted for several weeks after her death. It wasn't continuous though, they were just moments when the reality hit me. Sometimes it caught me totally off guard and other times it came on gradually. But it would leave almost as quickly as it arrived, then eventually it started to get less frequent. Much of the grief was not only in the fact that she had died but the way she had died. There is only one word that describes that whole event and that's 'horrific'. I don't think I have ever used that word to describe an event in my life, which is surprising really when you think about the previous chapters of this book. I think that is because during those times, I was the cause and I had lost my ability to feel. Years after these two life-changing events I ask myself which is the worse of the two? I can't answer that because they are so very different; one is my own suffering, the other is seeing someone else suffer. I don't have the answer to my own question right now but I expect it will come to me eventually.

My relationship with Carolyn, although 5,000 miles away, was going strong and in January of 2013 she offered to contribute to the cost of my ticket for a trip over there as it would help with my grief. On the second day of me arriving we went to her mum's house. I had done several trips leading up to this point and so was accustomed to their family way of life. I was very much into healthy eating and exercise but I was willing to relax my intense regime while I was away. This trip was much like the others, alcohol and food being the main focus. I was only there for a week and with the recent trauma of losing my mother it was easy to justify the 7-day party lifestyle.

Carolyn and her family were not the types to make the best of a situation and lacked motivation and zest for life in many aspects. Their lifestyle wasn't something I was particularly familiar with outside of my own self. My immediate family were the complete opposite. Daily exercise routines, healthy and mindful eating, socialising with friends and regular outings. As far as I'm concerned, that's the formula for a positive and balanced well-being. That is why I have always admired and continue to admire my family and strive to be just like them. There would be no greater compliment than for someone to say to me, 'you are just like your dad or your sister or your step-mum!' I know I am a way off that but it is something I am aiming for. They are such a positive influence in my life and indeed in the lives of people who meet them and get to know them.

It was just like any other day at Carolyn's mum's house. She was asleep in her chair in front of the TV. This was not only her chosen daytime activity after work but also her preferred sleeping area as she rarely actually slept in a bed. I could see exactly who was the biggest influence in Carolyn's life. She would also frequently stay up into the early hours of the morning, sometimes working on her Master's Degree in Couples Counselling, other times it was hours of mind-numbing reality dating shows. During my visits I would maintain a healthy routine as much as I could. Sleep is a big part of this and I suffer the following day if I do not get enough. Most of the time I would go to bed at my usual time, then Carolyn might come to bed hours later and inevitably wake me up. The days were mainly spent on my own. Carolyn's roommate would return home from work before her, and he and I would go to the bar across the street, have a couple of beers and share some mozzarella sticks with a side of marinara sauce for dipping. Jimmy never had any money so it was always down to me to be the provider. He was at least a bit of company and conversation, and we actually got along quite well together.

Jimmy and Carolyn had a strange relationship. She would mother him whenever she could and he appeared to be forever in debt to her. I mean emotionally, practically and financially indebted to her. There were subtle signs with their relationship that made me uncomfortable. Not so much that they once dated and were now apparently best friends (although I do not believe it is healthy to bring a past relationship into a present one), it was more of the submissive behaviour Jimmy would display to Carolyn, much like a dog that was desperate to please his owner and then roll onto his back in a pathetically weak manner.

He would make random visits from his bedroom, walk into the living room and say 'is there anything I can get for you, Carolyn?' She would respond with 'yes, please can you fill my wine glass?' And off he would then go to the kitchen and refill her glass to the very top with a red Merlot. This behaviour was not random, it was a constant. Two or three times in one evening he would appear from his bedroom and ask the same question. I always knew when he was about to appear as the waft of weed that followed straight after he had opened his bedroom door was intoxicating. I hate drugs. I always have. I've never even tried weed. I was given the opportunity many times when I was a teenager but I was too scared to try it then, but as I got older my reason for not trying shifted to knowing I would love it and wouldn't be able to stop at just one puff. I have since learned that obsessive behaviour is one of the characteristics of people who have been diagnosed with Borderline Personality Disorder. I was a visitor in their world and so I wasn't in a position to criticise Jimmy's chosen lifestyle of tobacco, alcohol and marijuana, but to be honest it did disgust me.

The day before I had to return to England was always very difficult. Carolyn and I knew it would be several months before we would see each other again and there was a very deep sense of dread that had a kick-start 24 hours before the actual event. Sadly, we had gotten used to these feelings as this was one of many trips we would make to see each other. As soon as we said our goodbyes, it was time to adjust back into my somewhat single life, that included much of the time only having to think about myself. I could still do exactly what I liked and when I liked. Grocery shopping for one, paying the bills for one, and so on.

My focus now was very much on improving myself, improving the aspect of my life I could control as I knew that is what would improve my well-being.

For the next few months I would continue with the healthy lifestyle, the exercise regime and socialising with family and friends. *Pets Alone* was doing very well too. I was busy walking dogs five days a week and so by the time the weekend came I was happy to relax. This was something I was having to learn how to do again as I had spent so many weekends in fear and isolation with time being my worst enemy. My relationship with weekends had changed. For a long time, Sundays were my least favourite day of the week and I was determined now to make it my favourite day of the week.

I wasn't able to take on more clients as I was working to full capacity. Although the work was tiring, it enabled me to put some money away each month so I could buy my next ticket to the USA and even perhaps save for a rainy day. Despite the somewhat unnerving behaviour I had encountered on my last visit, Carolyn and I were going strong and it was clear that we wanted to take our relationship further. We had only talked briefly about one of us moving so we could be together, and as the conversations progressed we had decided that if we ever had the opportunity then it would be me who would make the move across the ocean.

In June of 2013 DOMA or the Definition of Marriage Act was abolished in the USA. It was introduced by Bill Clinton in 1996 and defined marriage as being between one man and one woman. In 2013 this Act was challenged and rescinded by then President of the United States, Barack Obama. The Supreme Court then abolished the act, which opened the door for people of the same sex to legally marry in the United States. This meant that residency would also be granted for foreign nationals who wished to marry a US citizen. This of course was huge news for us and the possibility of me moving to the United States of America became a reality. Carolyn and I agreed that it would be me that would make the move. Of course, there were many factors that contributed to this decision but my circumstances were a better fit, I always felt so comfortable with the American way of life when I visited, like I was meant to be there. And frankly, the weather pattern of cold winters and hot summers was a breath of fresh air when compared to the long months of grey skies and uncertain sunshine in the UK.

I was mentally preparing for this being a reality and although there were many steps to take with great uncertainty, I fully committed myself to the process. Despite her different lifestyle, I wanted to spend the rest of my life with Carolyn and she told me she wanted to spend the rest of her life with me.

So we immediately began the long journey of paperwork in order to make our dream come true. Endless forms had to be completed, as well as evidence of our relationship, several hundred dollars had to be paid in fees until we were finally ready to send the application for processing.

In the meantime, we continued with our visits as often as we were able to. With work commitments and the financial burden of a transatlantic flight, it worked out about two or three times per year that we would see each other. Of course, we were also in regular contact via the internet, which meant that we could see and hear each other as if we were in the same room. One of the conditions of the 'Fiance Visa' was that we were required to marry each other within 90 days of me arriving in the country. This only added to the excitement at the possibility of us actually sharing the same space for more than 10 days.

I thought that Carolyn was very much a girlie girl, which for me was part of the attraction and so nothing gave her more pleasure than looking through endless magazines at engagement rings. I would be sent a lot of photos by text message to show me her favourites. I had been saving up for the ring and had given her a budget of $2,000. She called me one day and told me she had found the ring she really wanted, but that it would cost $4,000. Her insistence on having this particular ring fitted in with previous behaviour such as the constant requests for gifts, not just at Christmas, or for birthdays or Valentine's Day presents, but also requests for money to be spent on her and something bought for her from me. Up until this point I had given in to her unreasonable demands for 'stuff', but this was a whole new level of expenditure that I just wasn't willing or able to do. I said that I had saved hard for a ring up to the value of $2,000 and that I didn't have the means to pay any more. But because her desire to own this particular ring was so important to her, she offered to pay for half of it. Because I knew what it meant to her to have it, I agreed. It wasn't until a short time later that this had a profound effect on me. I had this feeling that I was not being good enough, not earning enough to provide her with the things she wanted. I had never heard of an instance where the bride paid for half of her engagement ring and it made me feel inadequate, so my self-esteem took a beating from it.

In September of 2013 I made another trip to Cleveland, Ohio. I had arranged for Carolyn's mum to collect me from the airport and take me straight to the jewellery store to collect the ring. Carolyn thought I was arriving the next day but me turning up on bended knee one day earlier than expected was all part of the surprise. It went without a hitch and was everything I had imagined it would be. We were engaged to be married and more excited than ever at the prospect of being together every day for the rest of our lives. Now it was a waiting game for the Department of Homeland Security to process our application. One of the stages was a medical report which had to be carried out by an authorised doctor. I was particularly nervous about the psychological evaluation, not because I was fragile at the time but because of my history. I fully disclosed my mental health and took a letter with me from my General Practitioner. I did feel that honesty really was the best policy. Despite the turbulent times it was clear to them that I had overcome my difficulties and was not going to be claiming medical benefits once in the United States.

The final stage of the process was an in-person interview at the American Embassy in London. It was my first time there and what an intimidating and daunting place it was, heavily guarded with armed security and access by appointment only. The interview itself took no more than 5 minutes. I was asked basic questions like, 'When did you and Carolyn first meet?' 'Where did you meet?' 'When did you last see each other?' 'What does she do for employment?' and so on.

The gentleman behind the screen asked for my passport and after a moment, congratulated me on being approved for my K1 Visa into the United States. I was on my way to a new life!

C h a p t e r   9

Making the biggest move of my life, both physically and emotionally.

MY VISA STATED THAT I had 90 days from date of issue in which to move myself physically, and emotionally, across the ocean and marry the girl I had fallen in love with four years previously.

The emotional journey had started many months before but now it was time to physically move. I had begun to put the wheels in motion prior to my application being approved. I met all the requirements for the immigrant visa and so I had put the word out that I was selling *Pets Alone* and selling the house that Barbara and I jointly owned. It was full steam ahead once I had received my passport back with my visa in. There were so many variables that had to fall correctly into place and there was no room for error.

Encouragingly, I had interest in *Pets Alone* fairly quickly, with several people asking about the operation of the business and wanting to learn more about income, number of customers and so on. Most of these enquiries only got so far then quickly and simply just vanished, but there was one who wanted to know more and seemed keen on obtaining more customers and expanding her own business. She was a friend of one of my customers who had a similar business of her own but on a smaller scale to mine.

The house was also on the market and the timing of both of these was crucial to me leaving for my new life. Despite Barbara not having contributed to the upkeep of the house that she was a joint owner of for almost 4 years, she was insistent she receive 50% of the equity. There were several viewings of our 3-bedroom, 3-storey town house and we received an offer fairly quickly for the asking price. There was no negotiation with Barbara and she knew that time wasn't on my side and I needed the house to sell in order to move. I had spoken to a friend of mine who had been married and divorced twice before.

She had told me that the first time she got divorced she fought for everything she could including his pension, property and cars etc. The second time she divorced she simply walked away and didn't fight. This story she told remained with me throughout the negotiation stage and I ended up giving in to Barbara's demands and told her she could have half of the equity. I was tired of fighting, not so much fighting Barbara but I had spent years fighting to stay alive and I was ready to embrace what I knew would now be 'my time'. I had absolutely no doubt at all that what I was doing was the right thing. After all the challenges I had faced and overcome I knew that I was doing the right thing in moving and starting a new life with Carolyn. I began to sell, give away and dump the entire contents of my house. I was able to get a little cash for electrical items but the majority of my possessions were given away to friends, family and charity shops.

I had decided I was only going to take what I could carry to America, but of course Hugo my chocolate Labrador would also have to come with me. I told myself that if Hugo wasn't going then neither was I.

The paperwork required in order to fly a domestic animal from England to the United States is endless. Coming from a rabies-free country and going to a country that has rabies is a process all on its own. Hugo had to have three vaccinations and all timed at precisely the correct day over a 6-week period. There was also the option of Hugo having his own passport. This would only prove to be useful if for whatever reason we would have to return to England. The pet passport meant that Hugo would not have to go into quarantine should we be faced with making a return journey.

I had finally received a deposit for the sale of *Pets Alone* and we had a date for the exchange of contracts on the house sale. Slowly but surely things were falling into place and there were fewer things I needed to find a home for. I was very sad to be moving away from *Pets Alone*. It had been a lifeline for me at times, not to mention the friends, both animal and human, I had made over the 7 years I was in business. I arranged that the new owner Cynthia would shadow me for the last week I was the owner of the company. This gave her an opportunity to get to know the dogs and their owners and for me to get authorisation from the owners to hand her their house keys. On March 27 2014 I finally handed over the keys to my clients as well as my trusty van to Cynthia, and from then on, I was unemployed and no longer the owner of *Pets Alone*.

On March 28 I handed over the keys to my house and a new family took ownership. So, I was now unemployed and homeless! There is a real sense of vulnerability when you have no possessions, no job and no home, but at the same time I found it quite liberating. I didn't have time to process the things I had lost, I was only able to look forward and think about the physical journey ahead and of getting Hugo safely to the United States. I had done extensive research before I booked our flight as I wanted to make sure Hugo would be safe and I would be able to be on the same flight as him. I had read horror stories about how the captain of an aircraft wasn't aware there were live animals on board and had not put any heating on in the hold of the aircraft which meant that consequently family pets had perished in the freezing temperatures. My anxiety on this one thing was huge but I always had faith and trust that I was doing the right thing.

Hugo and I moved into my sister's house for our last week in the country. I spent much of the time with my family and getting the last few things in order. Finances were a part of the closing stages of the journey, and with the sale of the house and *Pets Alone,* I had a little bit that would bring me comfort in the next chapter in my life. I hadn't been able to open a bank account of my own but Carolyn and I had opened a joint account on my last visit. At Carolyn's request, this was the only bank account either of us would have. Her salary was on a direct deposit straight into the account and I felt at ease transferring the majority of my monies into the account also. How easy it is to be wise in hindsight.

On April 10 2014 Dad rented a van. We needed the van as the requirements for Hugo's crate for the aircraft were very specific and very large. He and Jane arrived to pick me up at 8 o'clock in the morning. Eve and my two little nieces came out to see us off. I sat in the back of the van with two suitcases and Hugo. All the months of preparation had finally come down to this one moment of saying goodbye. The gut-wrenching emptiness and loss I felt at that moment was enormous. It covered every fibre of my body. The 'what if's' then crept into my mind but quickly got pushed away by the 'it's your time, Sammie, nothing can go wrong now'.

The journey to Heathrow went by quickly. We had to check Hugo into the cargo area 3 hours before the flight. To add to the stress, we had by necessity had to arrive half an hour before the cargo department opened, so we had to kick our heels and try to stay strong. This was naturally the moment I had dreaded for so many months. As I handed over the paperwork to the lady behind the desk I asked where Hugo would be kept until he boarded the plane. She explained that since 9/11 the rules had changed concerning the transportation of goods and animals. Consequently, I was required to put him into the crate and was only able to let him out once we had arrived in New York. My heart sank. I had wrongly assumed he would have a grass area and a nice kennel and be loaded onto the plane moments before departure. My eyes filled up and my stomach felt empty, but I still knew that ultimately this was still the right thing for me to do. My new, happy life was so close. We just had to get through this final stage. Hugo was in the crate with a couple of his favourite toys that included his much loved 'birthday cake' and a teddy he had from when he was just 8 weeks old. At the very last minute I ran to the van, got my pyjama top from my bag and threw it into the crate. Two guys appeared, lifted the crate onto a pallet and a fork lift truck came and carried the pallet, the crate and my Hugo off into the warehouse. My heart and my body were both heavy with fear, dread and with guilt at what I was putting Hugo through. I had to trust that he would be fine and that I would see him at the other end. The only way I was going to be able to mentally cope with the anxiety of not knowing how he was or even if he was alive was to block him and the situation out of my mind.

The next wave of emotions came immediately. Finally, it was time to say goodbye to Dad and Jane. I experienced a second wave of intolerable gut-wrenching, heart-sinking sadness. I asked myself one last time if this was what I wanted to do. But I immediately answered with a confident yes. It was my time. Hugo was going to be fine, I would spend the rest of my life with Carolyn, I had no doubts at all. It was time to be practical. I had to get myself onto the plane and maintain some sort of composure, all the while trying to achieve the goal of landing myself and Hugo safely in New York. Being on the plane over the Atlantic and wondering how Hugo was doing was expectedly one of the hardest things I have ever had to do. Every sound was amplified as was every bump. I had to block it out and pretend it wasn't happening.

Nine hours later we arrived at New York. I approached the customs counter and showed them my Visa and passport. I was immediately taken to another room where I was asked questions about my relationship with Carolyn. After a tense 30 minutes, my passport was stamped and I was allowed entry into the United States. I picked up my two bags from the baggage reclaim and headed towards the exit where Carolyn was pulling in to pick me up. We hadn't seen each other for several months and I should have been relieved, excited and thrilled that I had made it. But that was overshadowed by my being desperate to get to Hugo. I was told he was in the cargo area and that was where I needed to go. We drove around for 20 minutes trying to find the place and when we eventually did, I then had to take a seat in a waiting area. I could see Hugo's giant crate just down the hall. My heart was pounding. Although I knew he was just there I wasn't able to go to him as I needed paperwork in order for him to clear customs. I collected the necessary paperwork and the address to where I needed to take it. Another 20 minutes trying to find this location and another wait in line. Finally, I handed over the paperwork and was told Hugo had cleared customs and I was free to collect him. Back we went over to the other side of the airport where I would finally be reunited with him.

As I approached his crate I got down onto his level and spoke to him in my high-pitched, comforting mummy voice. I opened the door to the crate but he was too terrified to come out. I climbed in to get him and coax him out. I had to carry him outside to the nearest grass area so he could pee. I think he was relieved by this but at the same time terrified at the surroundings and the ordeal of the journey. We loaded up the car with my bags, a huge crate and Hugo, and drove to a dog friendly hotel in Queens, New York City. I put water out for Hugo as soon as we got to the room and he gulped down 2 big bowls. That night we were both restless and both had jet lag. I took him for a short walk several times during the night and as he and I roamed the streets of New York at 2am the enormity of what we had been through really hit me. The next day, it was a 6-hour drive to Cleveland, Ohio, which would be our home and our new family and life together. Carolyn had two Boston terriers as well as her -ex who was also still living with her. Rather strange, I thought.

The first couple of weeks were spent getting Hugo settled and used to his new environment. I could see the journey had taken its toll on him and he appeared to have aged from it. As we got more comfortable and continued with the adjustment, Carolyn and I started to make plans for our marriage. Because there were conditions to my visa it took away a large part of the romantic element to a marriage. Although we both knew we wanted to be with each other for the rest of our lives, being dictated to about when and where we needed to marry was a disappointment and a struggle. The state of Ohio didn't recognise or perform same sex marriages, and so we were required to go out of state to get the job done. Carolyn had found a bed and breakfast place that was 'gay friendly' in the town of Findley Lake in New York State. We took the 2-hour car journey on the Friday and Carolyn's mum and step-dad came the following day.

The ceremony took place just outside of the B and B on Findley Lake. It was a beautiful setting and took approximately 10 minutes to perform. Immediately afterwards I was overcome with emotion. Much of it was because my mum wasn't there, in fact I didn't have any family there, and that was hard. The other part of the tears was the relief of having finally made it. The US visa process is lengthy, costly and emotionally trying, but all the pieces had finally come together. We were finally married and ready to start our new life together.

Chapter 10

Life is not a bed of roses, especially when your beliefs about someone are shattered. But I survive.

WE WERE HAPPY AS CAN be. I had a bit of money from the sale of *Pets Alone* and the house and we celebrated for the first three months of me arriving. We were married and very much in love. We ate and drank and had a great time. We were also wanting to set up home and so we spent some money on a new couch, which was my idea. Carolyn wanted a new mattress for the bed, at $3,000. I reluctantly agreed.

I sat down to do the finances as I was wanting to put an end to our spending. Having been financially irresponsible in the past I was not going to let that happen again. Carolyn had asked me if it was okay if we made one last payment to the finance company for her engagement ring. The deal was that she was going to make all payments before I moved here. Feeling vulnerable at my situation I agreed to this also.

Carolyn is very dedicated to her work and her school studies. Her working days are long and when she does eventually return home she spends a lot of her time working on her Master's Degree in Couples Counselling, and when she has free time it is spent either sleeping or watching TV. There is a definite pattern forming of coming home from work, watching TV for several hours, falling asleep on the couch then working on her studies until the early hours of the morning. When she does eventually come to bed at about 3am, she is loud! I'm not sure if this fits in with the American stereotype or if it's a characteristic of Carolyn alone.

Moving from one country to another is an enormously emotional experience made up of several components. The process is dominated by the thoughts of what you have given up, i.e. family, friends, job etc. It's easy to be consumed by this alone but in fact there are many other elements to the transition process such as the unfamiliarity, the vulnerability, the feeling of isolation. For the first few months I felt like a child again. Grocery shopping was a long and frustrating process, you don't realise how much of a successful shopping trip is based on what our eyes are familiar with. We spend years buying the same brand of butter, milk, yoghurt, cheese etc, then all of a sudden you are faced with endless decisions that start with 2%, soy, half and half, sharp Cheddar, whipped butter, and what should take you seconds ends up being a major event with many mistakes along the way!

I was hoping for some help and guidance from Carolyn and her family in the everyday tasks and the challenge of establishing myself Stateside. I had to get a social security card which is a legal requirement, and I had to take a driving test before I could get my license. Unfortunately, I was left to carry out the research myself on all aspects which was disappointing and at times hurtful. There seemed to be no appreciation of the enormity of my situation.

I wasn't able to work for the first 6 months after arriving in the country because of visa restrictions but as soon as I was legally able, I started looking for a job. In the meantime, I contributed any way I could by keeping the house clean and tidy and making meals for Carolyn and me and also Jimmy when he was taking a break from his diet of nicotine, marijuana and *Budweiser*. I had the time to spend on making nice meals and I brought some of my culinary skills with me and made some apparently interesting dishes that Carolyn and Jimmy had never tasted. I enjoyed my daily walks with Hugo and Carolyn's Boston Terriers, although they clearly hadn't been socialised or trained and so were very hard work all of the time.

My next-door neighbour whom I had got close with came down to the house one day and brought with her a newspaper cutting with an advert for a dog handler for a goose control company. I had never heard of such a thing but the possibility of working outside with dogs was very appealing. It was advertised as part-time which I was happy with at the time while I continued with the transition. It also meant I would still be able to spend time with Hugo.

I applied for the position online and received a phone call from the HR department of the privately-owned company soon afterwards. The lady I spoke to had an accent which was comforting in a way as she too was not American born or so I was assuming. I wasn't able to get any further along in the interview process until I had got my Ohio driving license so the following day I got to work on it. I was fortunate enough to pass the written and the practical test first time and the examiner actually made the comment that I was better than most Americans she had tested!

I immediately called the company to announce I had got my license and that I was excited at the possibility of working for them. I met with the owners of the company in a café and was taken aback at how relaxed and friendly they both were. It seemed like a perfect fit for what I was looking for and what I needed. I had some anxiety of going into a 9 to 5 office job because I knew mentally, I wouldn't be able to maintain that long-term. In the UK my anxiety issues had often run in tandem with my depression, and I didn't want to risk that returning. Over my recovery I had learned that my ability to cope with pressure was something that needed to be worked on, so for now this position couldn't be any more perfect.

I was delighted when I heard I had got the position of Dog Handler and I couldn't wait to get started. My first shift was in the evening and the owner gave me directions for the first client. "You take 90 then get on 71." I looked at him with a blank face. I had no idea what '90' was or indeed what '71' was! It turned out these were the numbers for the local highways. Needless to say, it was a good job the car was equipped with a GPS unit!

As I picked up more and more shifts I was getting closer to a full working week. I was also learning more about the company culture, the other staff members and the operation of the business. Using highly trained border collies successfully to humanely harass and chase Canada geese from properties was such a unique and interesting line of work. I loved having the opportunity to talk to people about my work. I found I had such passion in how I talked about it, not just about the work but also the company, the staff and the owners whom I was getting closer to on a personal level. I revelled in the opportunity to share my increasing knowledge of Canada geese and what I now did for a living.

My only disappointment was at the little or no interest I had from Carolyn. She didn't seem to want to know about my job or how my day was. It was clear the disappointments were getting more frequent in many areas of both of our lives. But I continued to maintain the home and make sure Carolyn had a cooked meal when she returned from work. I always asked her what time I should expect her to return from work but she was never able to stick to her original timing, nor did she communicate to tell me she would be late. Inevitably many meals I had cooked got thrown away because she had picked something up on her way home as it was so late. At weekends when she wasn't working I would plan to make a nice meal or had already made it but when it came to sitting down and eating I was then told that at that moment she had decided to be a vegan. I knew she was a vegetarian at times but to sporadically decide to be vegan was news to me. It was also difficult to understand how her eating habits were not consistent and by now I never knew if today she was a carnivore, a vegetarian or a vegan, and that determined whether she would eat the food I had made and put in front of her. This, coupled with the consistent non-arrival at pre-advised times made me wonder why I continued to make the effort and so I stopped. I made meals for myself and Carolyn managed her own eating plan.

With her haphazard schedule becoming more apparent, there were more planned occasions which were missed or that I was kept waiting for. After so many months of being let down because she didn't show up to an event, forgot or was too late for us to attend, I wondered why I continued to make the effort. As I was forming close friendships through work and also with the neighbours, I started spending more and more time with them.

Carolyn had a friend over to visit for an evening, and as we were sitting enjoying a drink Ally asked if it would be okay if she stayed with us for three to four months. Quite frankly I couldn't think of anything worse, but Carolyn thought it would be a great idea and said yes on the spot, and then said, "Is that okay with you, Sammie?" How could I refuse? Ally was moving out of state to be with her boyfriend and needed somewhere to stay during the transition. So a couple of weeks later, just four months after I arrived in the country and three months after we got married, not only did we have Jimmy but we now had Ally living with us and it was getting crowded. Paraphrasing a famous phrase used by Diana, Princess of Wales, I felt that there were now four of us in this marriage!

All three bedrooms in the rented house were occupied and so I had no choice but to be woken every night by Carolyn coming to bed, and again when she fell asleep and started snoring along with one of her Boston Terriers who was louder than most people due to his squashed nose cavity. The winter of 2015 was particularly bad with endless days of temperatures in the negative digits. It's the type of cold that hurts when you go outside. Day in and day out it was hard to maintain normality, particularly when it came to walking the dogs. Hugo couldn't understand why some days he wasn't getting a walk. Ever since I bought him at eight weeks old we had walked twice a day, but now there were days when it was too dangerous to go out for more than a few minutes because of the risk of frostbite. I would also learn that the postal workers were issued with goggles to stop their eyeballs from freezing! All very different from where I was brought up, where we considered an outside temperature of minus 3 Centigrade to be incredibly cold!

Carolyn's mum lived in the family home from 40 years ago when she was married to Carolyn's dad. Although she was just about able to keep up with the mortgage payments, any repairs or maintenance that needed doing were not carried out. With fewer opportunities in life, they were both working in minimum wage jobs.

Carolyn asked me again if we could make another payment from the joint account. This time it was to be a $2,000 loan to her mum to have a new boiler/furnace installed as she had no heat. I couldn't refuse. It was freezing and I couldn't stand the thought of anyone not being warm in the Ohio winter. It was a loan, so it would be repaid at some point. Or so I thought.

Sometime later I am somewhat surprised to get an email from Carolyn's sister Shania who had moved back to the USA. It doesn't make for pleasant reading. In fact, it is upsetting and very one-sided. She talks about how can I screw things up between Carolyn and me when we fought so hard to get me here. Apparently, I constantly remind Carolyn that I gave up everything to be with her and that I am finding excuses for our marriage not to work. In addition, she is sorry for me that I don't have the close relationship with my family that she and Carolyn do!

I find this very difficult to digest. Her sister should not have such knowledge, false or true, of our marriage and she also should not be expressing her disgust and anger at me when she has only received one side of our marital problems. This email is not helpful and has actually put a greater wedge between Carolyn and me as well as her sister. Carolyn explains she was not aware her sister was sending me this email.

I was counting down the days until Ally left simply so I could move into the spare bedroom and get some much-needed undisturbed sleep. The house we rented was through a friend of Carolyn's whom she used to work with. There was no tenancy agreement and so everything was left very casual. One evening we all got a high-pitched alarm on our cell phones and an emergency message saying there was a tornado warning in place and to take cover. This was one of the few times I actually felt quite useless, because tornadoes in England are extremely rare. Carolyn and Jimmy were busy running around the house turning off all the electrical sockets and gathering all the dogs and Jimmy's cat as we were to make our way into the basement since underground is the safest place to be during a tornado. We had a battery powered radio, so we could tune into the local news for the weather updates. We were there for about an hour before it was safe to return upstairs.

As a result, I've discovered I'm not a fan of basements. There are typically no windows and many are not what they refer to as 'finished' which includes carpeting, painted walls and a comfortable living space. If it is finished then that is a bonus. I feel closed in without being able to see outside.

Finally, Ally had moved out to start her new life in Wisconsin and so I immediately moved into the bedroom. I was so relieved to now enjoy some good undisturbed sleep. In March of 2015 it was my 40th birthday. It's a big one and I have always been a fan of birthdays. I was excited at the prospect of a special trip or a party to celebrate. Rightly or wrongly I had hinted that as this was a special birthday, I would really like a new *iPad Mini*. My laptop was old and very slow and I needed something I could start up in a couple of minutes to video call family and friends back home. I wouldn't normally have been as upfront as this but thought that as it was a special birthday, she might like a present suggestion.

On the morning of my birthday I was presented with a small gift bag and inside were a couple of chocolate bars and some chewing gum. Carolyn was then rushing off to work and I waited with excited anticipation to see what her main gift would be. When she returned from work, she asked if I would like to go to the *Apple* store. Yes, yes, yes of course, I would! After we had walked around the store admiring the latest tech, Carolyn then asked if I was ready to leave. I was somewhat surprised but reluctantly agreed to leave empty-handed. I then suggested a meal out. Without that suggestion it seemed I would be getting two chocolate bars and some chewing gum for my birthday. As we sat down to dinner, I asked her what her intention was as far as the trip to the *Apple* store was concerned, and she explained she just thought it would be nice to walk around. As much as I tried, I couldn't hide my hurt and disappointment. It brought tears to my eyes to think she thought this was okay. Obviously, my comment about the *iPad Mini* had just not registered or had been ignored. Inevitably it ended badly and we returned home eating half a dinner.

I went into my bedroom and she went into hers. Shortly afterwards she burst into my room with an envelope and said, "Your birthday gift was a number of letters from friends and family saying what they loved about you, but only one person responded to my email requesting the letters." The envelope was thrown at me and she slammed the door and returned back to her room. There was just one letter and that was from my dear Dad. I briefly read it and wept. I haven't read it since but I have kept it. I don't feel able to read it again as it will be a clear reminder of that horrible evening.

With the events of the day, this added to our already tense and failing marriage. My work became my sanctuary. Working outside alone with the dog was exactly what I needed and so I was the first one to volunteer for any opportunity to take on extra shifts. In the summer of 2015, I took a short break and used my phone to log into the bank account to see where we stood with our finances. I panicked at what I saw as the joint savings account had been cleared out leaving just $1,000. That meant that $10,000 had been withdrawn. I immediately called Carolyn with huge concern. She explained she had opened her own bank account into which her salary was now going, and she had transferred the $10,000 from our joint account into hers as she felt insecure about us and wanted to protect herself. I was in total disbelief at what I was hearing. I had never felt so vulnerable in all of my life. At this point I didn't even have enough funds to get me back to England, which at that moment was exactly where I wanted to be. Later that day I asked her about it again and she said the same thing over and over again, "I am protecting myself." There was no way of getting the money back and I had to accept that I was now on my own in this and I had to do all I could to get myself financially stable. Her actions put an even greater strain on the marriage and we got to the point where we decided to go for counselling. Imagine, a couples' counsellor going for counselling!

I tried so hard to understand her rationale for taking the money and to try to see past it for the sake of our marriage. This was the main topic of discussion in the counselling session. I should also add that Carolyn said she was feeling attacked in the counselling session and refused to carry on. I decided to continue with the sessions alone as I was still trying to see things from Carolyn's perspective in the hope of saving our marriage.

In May of 2015 Carolyn decided she wanted to buy her first home. I knew I didn't want any part of the purchase. I certainly didn't want to be on the documents or have any financial interest that she was connected with. But I was excited that a new place might mean a fresh start for the both of us.

Samantha in contemplative mood.

Chapter 11

Emailing Obama! I finally realise just what I have got myself into… and need to get out of.

DESPITE ALL THE DIFFICULTIES WITH my relationship, there was one thing I was sure about. I loved the lifestyle in America, and had made the decision that whatever the outcome with Carolyn, I intended to stay and build a new life for myself. I was so grateful to the President the law that I decided on a whim to email him! I went onto the website of the White House and clicked on the 'Contact us' button. I typed a short three-line message, simply saying thank you. There was a 2-minute video showing the process for the thousands of pieces of mail they receive each week. They are filtered down to just three pieces a day which the President responds to and, incredibly, I was informed that mine was going to be one of them! I almost deleted their email response as spam, but then realised that this was a genuine reply to my hurried message. What a privilege to receive a personal response from the then President of the United States. It gave me a much-needed confidence boost. Having endured months of feeling worthless while living with Carolyn, this made me feel worthy and capable of anything. The President's email is now framed and has pride of place in my living room, and occasionally I will read it if I need that little 'I am worthy' top-up.

Here is what President Obama wrote to me:

Dear Samantha

Thank you for writing. Your story is an important part of our Nation's journey forward on the path toward LGBT equality.

The progress we've witnessed over the last few years is the result of countless acts of courage by people who came out, spoke out, and believed in themselves and who they were—and I am proud of how far our country has come. Still, work remains to ensure all our people, regardless of who they are or who they love, can realize America's promise. Our Nation's narrative is one that has been written by dedicated citizens who have proven throughout history that with persistence, we can build a more tolerant, more inclusive society. As long as passionate individuals like you continue stepping up in defense of the rights and freedoms of all Americans, I am confident our progress will continue.

Again, thank you for writing. Messages like yours inspire me to keep doing everything I can to ensure America is a place where all people can live freely and shape their own destiny.

Sincerely,
Barack Obama

ON THANKSGIVING OF 2015, CAROLYN'S mum and step-dad were over to enjoy the celebration. The food was piled high and the drinks were flowing. When Carolyn drank it had the complete opposite effect on me and made me want to stay away from it. It became apparent I was not drinking alcohol for weeks at a time.

By noon, Carolyn had consumed several drinks and you could see the effects taking place. As she looked out of the window, she saw her mum and step-dad pull up into the driveway. She was excited at their arrival and rushed out of the front door to greet them. In doing so, she fell down the steps and into the flower bed, apparently hurting herself as the incident made her cry. I did my best to be sympathetic but internally was cringing and keeping my own thoughts to myself.

When she had been drinking she seemed to get childlike in her actions and conversation. Her excitement for the occasion was not controlled as it should be when you're a grown woman and this just reminded me of her frequent comment of 'I hate being an adult'. Before dinner was served there was a video call with her sister in Nebraska. She and her husband had recently had a baby and so the conversation was dominated with 'baby talk'. I found it difficult to talk with her sister as I was still in shock over the email she had sent months earlier. As we served the traditional Thanksgiving dinner Carolyn was overcome with emotion and openly cried at the table. When asked what the matter was, she said that she was sad because she so desperately wanted children and the conversation with her sister had triggered that thought. It was in our plan to have children as part of 'living the dream' but I had told her previously I was not prepared to make any more major commitments to her until we had a good solid and happy six months of living together.

With Carolyn in tears for the second time that day, it made for a tense afternoon and I couldn't help but think her behaviour was exacerbated by the alcohol. One typical trait of her drinking was that she became even more controlling than usual. As I walked through the doorway from the kitchen into the living room she jumped in front of me and spread out her arms blocking the entryway. "You're not coming through until you kiss me," she said. I tried to laugh but it was clear this was one of the most uncomfortable moments in my life. She then went to grab my crotch and my breast and repeated, "You're not coming through until you kiss me." Kissing her was the furthest thing from my mind and I actually wanted to push her out of the way. But in order to avoid further discomfort with our guests, I reached over and kissed her gently and quickly. The 'barrier' went up and I was free to go into the living room.

Her persistent grabbing of me inappropriately in front of her parents made me unbearably uncomfortable. I made the excuse that I didn't feel too well and took myself off upstairs and into my bedroom. I was thinking about the day's events and as I started to process and try to make sense of it I realised my wife made me feel like I had been violated. I had said 'no' several times to her demands but that was not an option. I climbed into bed and decided I had given enough thought to the situation and needed some distraction. I used the small screen on my phone to watch some mindless television and eventually fell asleep. But at 3am she entered my bedroom drunk and wanted to have sex, so I pretended to still be asleep until she eventually gave up and went to her own room.

The following morning, I was miserable and still feeling physically violated. It was a heavy, thick feeling that I wasn't used to. I was questioning myself over and over about how I could have handled it differently, but I felt like I had no choice. Being so far away from home with no funds and still building a support network of friends, I worried that Carolyn was capable of throwing me out onto the street and that was a very real fear.

I was so grateful for my work and I put every hour in I could, not just because it was an escape from my home life, but I knew there was potential to climb up in the company. In my annual performance review, I was presented with an offer to change my role within the company from Dog Handler to Account Manager. This was the moment I had been working towards and it was an opportunity not to be missed. They told me I would be responsible for starting up the company in Ohio's capital city Columbus, but at the same time I would continue to be a dog handler for 2 days a week. Of course, I accepted the position and got to work immediately. Carolyn, however, was unable to congratulate me or be happy for my promotion. Yet another disappointment. This was unfamiliar territory for me. I was having to learn the American way of doing business, the do's and don'ts as well as the regular 130-mile trips to Columbus on a weekly basis. But I thrived on the opportunity and the vision of further progression within the company.

Things between Carolyn and me were not getting any better and she seemed to be drinking more than ever. I was still prepared and desperately trying to save our marriage and I would sporadically try to start a conversation to see if we could sort things out. Because of her haphazard schedule I never knew when this would take place and so it was never planned. I spoke to Carolyn about the consistent lateness or 'no show' when we had arranged a date or a night out with friends and she responded with 'I can't commit to being home at a certain time and sticking to it and so I'm not going to give you a time'. She also admitted that at times when we were not getting along she was deliberately unkind to me, being loud when she went to bed to wake me up, slamming the door on the microwave or deciding to move furniture around at 3 o'clock in the morning. This felt like a slap in the face with zero effort on her part and no acknowledgment of how this looked and its effect on our relationship. I was immediately left disappointed with her attitude but was told I shouldn't be and in fact I should praise her for trying. I was left stunned at this comment and inevitably I started to distance myself and spend more and more time with my friends who were able to commit to arrangements. I was so motivated to explore my new surroundings, be outside and enjoy everything that my new home had to offer.

One day Carolyn had called in sick and didn't go to work and so was in the house when I returned from work. She failed to realise I had returned home and carried on with the video call with her sister. "You should divorce her sooner rather than later, as she will try to take half of everything." "She's so boring, she goes to bed at 9 o'clock, she's no fun." These are just two of the things I overheard in that conversation.

In January of 2016 I decided I could no longer put off making an appointment with my doctor about a lump I had found in my breast. I was referred for a mammogram. Three kind people offered to accompany me to the appointment but not one of those people was my wife, nor did she ask me how my appointment went. There was no interest, concern or compassion for any aspect of my life. It turned out it wasn't cancer but I needed a second appointment to have the lump aspirated. I didn't tell Carolyn about that appointment as my thought process was if she didn't have the information that I was going then I couldn't be disappointed when she failed to ask me about it, and I couldn't handle yet another disappointment. As it turned out the lump was benign and no further treatment was needed. As I left the hospital I couldn't help but think how many people left from a similar appointment but with a totally different outcome. I was feeling very lucky.

Some time later I was overjoyed to hear that Dad and Jane were going to make a trip to visit me in Cleveland, and in early May of 2016 they arrived for a one week stay. Dad and Jane like their comforts and were happy to stay in a good local hotel which I found for the duration of their visit. Although they had an insight into what was going on in my home life, I never expected they would experience it first-hand. They had organised an evening out for a meal followed by a concert by the Cleveland Orchestra. I had spent the day with Dad and Jane shopping in the local mall and we all made the short journey back to the house to change and collect Carolyn. At 5pm she was still in bed sleeping. Dad and Jane seemed somewhat surprised at this but for me it was a regular occurrence and expected, so I took her up a cup of tea and gently woke her up. I reiterated our earlier conversation that we had to leave by six to make it on time. At 5.45 she had still not made it out of bed. She finally appeared at twenty past six. This made for a stressful situation as we had to rush to get downtown for the meal I had booked at 6.30pm. Of course, we were late and hurried our food in order to get to the concert on time. Carolyn couldn't resist making the comment, "You drive like my grandma, put your foot down." I was not prepared to drive fast to be unsafe in order not to miss the beginning of the concert, because her frustration was actually caused by her own actions of not getting out of bed. Inevitably we missed the first 10 minutes of the concert and had to stand at the back until the interval. Dad had secured front row seats for us, so the long walk down the aisle in the interval was also embarrassing.

As Dad and Jane were always trying to do the best for me, they suggested a crisis meeting with Carolyn, her mother and step-father. The meeting was set up for a couple of days later and took place in the house in Cleveland. Carolyn and her family were on one side of the room and me and my family on the other. Carolyn went straight into attack mode and laid out all the things I had apparently said and done during our short marriage. One point particularly stood out that came from her mother was the fact that early on in my arrival in the United States I had called Carolyn immoral. I didn't elaborate on this at the time but would like to take the opportunity to do so now. When I questioned Carolyn about her alcohol consumption when she was driving, she actually stated that the drink drive limit in Ohio was set according to the average size person and she was not the average size so was able to consume more and therefore the law didn't apply to her! That behaviour to me is immoral.

The attacks kept coming but I didn't rise to them. The conclusion of the uncomfortable meeting was that we were going to give our marriage one last shot. Carolyn took some convincing to get to this agreement but I knew in my heart that this really was it. The next day Dad and Jane returned home, so I was once again on my own trying to sort out the mess I had got into.

In July of the same year my boss and their family went on vacation for three weeks and asked me to move into their beautiful home to look after the working dogs, the house and the business while they were away. I was flattered that they trusted me with this responsibility, and the time leading up to this point was spent waiting for it to arrive. I couldn't wait to have peace, tranquillity and a good night's sleep. I was relying on the break from Carolyn to bring us back together when we reunited. Almost immediately into the three weeks I felt a new sense of calm. I found that only being responsible for myself (and a pack of border collies!) created a feeling I had never experienced. Combined with my general well-being I was indulging in the new space that was created in my brain. It made me realise just how chaotic my day-to-day living with Carolyn had become. There was no need for television, music or even socialisation. The new, empty mental space partly created by the beautiful surroundings was all the entertainment I needed. I spent hours just sitting in complete silence simply enjoying the tranquillity. But I knew this wasn't permanent and towards the end of the three weeks I had to prepare to return to my life with Carolyn. I was hoping she had used the time like me to reflect on herself and us.

I now knew what life could be like every day and I so hoped this could be recreated once I returned home. It was a new start but also the final attempt to save our marriage. My relationship with Carolyn's family had been rocky at times and I knew my efforts would need to include her family members also, so I immediately got to work on strengthening relationships. Her sister would soon be visiting and staying with us for a week and so I took the opportunity to have a heart to heart with her. I was nervous as I knew there were things that needed to be included in the conversation. I expressed my upset at what had been said to Carolyn and overheard by me, and I needed to let her know so she could work on that side of our relationship. The meeting went well and there was huge relief on both sides.

The next opportunity was with Carolyn's mum. There was a hot air balloon festival a one hour drive out of the city and I thought this would be the perfect opportunity to show both of them that I was serious in my efforts to save my marriage.

We started the drive to the east side of the city. The next task was to find a parking place. The road closure was set up approximately three miles away from the venue. Carolyn drove into a resident's driveway and suggested we park there and walk. The confused and inquisitive resident appeared from the house and asked what we were doing on his property. Carolyn, instead of asking politely, merely suggested it wouldn't be a problem for us to use his land to park and start the three mile walk to the festival. The resident looked as stunned and surprised as I was in the car cringing with embarrassment at the situation. He reluctantly agreed and we set off in the dark on the unlit country road. Not long into our walk a black *BMW* pulled over and offered us a ride. Carolyn and Maggie jumped at the opportunity not to have to endure the long walk. The three of us squeezed into the back of the car, enjoying the feel of the leather seats. The venue for the balloon festival was a vineyard which wasn't without anxiety on my part, because it just meant there was more wine for Carolyn to choose from. Overwhelmed by the vast array of fine wines, she was unable to decide which one to buy so bought two bottles of equally aged Merlot. It was a long wait for the festival to get underway and the wind meant there would be no flights but instead the balloons would remain tethered. This still made for a beautiful sight in the dark skies. Carolyn was well into her second bottle when it was time to leave. Knowing we had a long drive home, coupled with my desire to remain in control meant I didn't drink and I stuck to soft drinks all evening. Carolyn commented that I was boring and no fun to be with. I ignored her comments as much as I could but I could feel my anxiety setting in as I knew we had a three mile walk back to the car. At 11pm at the close of the festival we started the trek. Carolyn flagged down a car with two ladies and asked if we could get a ride. They happily agreed. The three of us climbed into the compact car. There was an overwhelming smell of marijuana in the car and both the passenger and the driver were taking regular hits. The joint was passed to the back of the car and Carolyn enjoyed a puff or two. She then offered it to me, which I naturally declined. Having inherited an addictive nature from my mother I generally abstain from any activity that might be habit-forming.

Carolyn offered the joint to her mother who also declined. I was in disbelief at what I was witnessing. The driver of the vehicle asked if they party like this in England. Before I could conjure up an appropriate response Carolyn took the lead and informed everyone that I was British and boring and didn't know how to have fun. The torment didn't end there. I was feeling bullied and vulnerable, something I had not experienced since my school days. The erratic journey of the clearly stoned driver was also terrifying, but I got to the stage where I was willing the near miss of the side ditch to be a full-on collision, because this would at least end the verbal bullying I was enduring from my wife and two strangers. Fortunately, the car journey was short and I couldn't have jumped out of the car any faster.

I could immediately feel this experience had reached a part of my soul. It was deep and mentally scarring. I walked the last remaining yards to the car several paces ahead of Carolyn and Maggie. At this point I wanted to get far away from them. I had to hold it together as we had a long journey home. When faced with challenging situations I close myself to the outside, then focus and listen to my mind, processing every thought and feeling as it comes. This means I am silent until I am required to engage in the outside world. Once we arrived home I immediately went to my bedroom and shut down for the night. This disappointment at how my efforts to rebuild my relationship with Carolyn's family and the response I got was the final straw.

The following morning the acute pain of the evening's events had ever so slightly lessened, but the thought of spending the day with Carolyn and

Maggie at a pre-arranged family gathering made me feel physically unwell. While Carolyn was still in bed I called my boss and asked her if she needed me to work that day. Although it was a Saturday I knew that working would be a reasonable justification for me not to have to attend the family event. The response to my request from my boss was that there was actually no need for me to work that day, but when I insisted and knowing some of the history of my volatile relationship she simply said, "Yes, we need you to work today!" That wasn't the first time I turned to my job as an escape from my relationship. Working outside with the dogs chasing Canada geese had been my go-to place several times and there was nothing else I would rather be doing at that moment.

As the days passed, I could feel myself beginning to accept that this might be the end of the relationship. Before I made any impulsive decisions, I needed to give myself time to heal from the experience of that night. Carolyn and I sat down together and talked. Yet again she reminded me what a good person she was, how she liked herself and didn't need to change. She told me she wanted me to put her on a pedestal and treat her like a princess. Personally, I can't think of anything worse than being put on a pedestal by my significant other. I don't want to be held in higher regard but on the same level. With all of the events over the last two and a half years I knew I was not able to fulfil her request. We had tried so many times to meet each other's needs but this time I was not able to and I knew it. It was finally agreed that our marriage was over, and I should immediately look for somewhere else to live.

As time went on I would mentally revisit the events at the festival, and I eventually became thankful it had happened. It was the kicker I needed in order to accept the end of our life together. I immediately got to work on searching for an apartment where Hugo and I would feel happy and safe, and in the meantime the details of the dissolution were being negotiated. I literally had nothing to take with me that was mine to set up a home with, and the smallest of possessions such as spoons and plates had to be fought for and recorded on a legal document. I confronted Carolyn one evening as she laid on the couch in the basement watching TV. I requested several small but practical items that I could take with me. When she responded with 'no, you can't take anything, not even a tea spoon', I asked her if she had any sympathy for my situation. Her response was one of the most hurtful I have ever received from anyone my entire life. "I never asked you to move here," she said. This was when I experienced the death of expectation. Again, like the physical experiences she had made me endure, this got right into my soul.

Over the years, I have discovered that I rarely get angry at other people but instead I get desperately sad. This, however, caused me to momentarily lose my shit (a common American term!) and I punched the wall as I made my way back into the house from the basement. Maybe I still wasn't angry with her but with myself for making what was apparently the wrong decision in committing myself physically, emotionally and financially to her. Yes, she had taken me financially and physically, but the most important aspect was emotionally. Being vulnerable to extreme emotions which can cause me to act impulsively means I have to keep myself in check. Every minute of every day the health of my brain is a priority, and I knew this new situation was going to be a test.

Chapter 12

A tough moment, but as one door closes... and I start to understand my mental rehabilitation.

AFTER WHAT SEEMED LIKE A lifetime of searching for an apartment I could afford, I finally found a place I knew I would be happy in, in a nice town about 20 minutes west of downtown Cleveland. With the help of friends once again, I brought Hugo and my meagre possessions into the ground floor apartment and set about building a new life for myself.

Moving day was hectic. I was fortunate to have a couple of friends help me with getting the large items into the truck I had rented. Despite Carolyn's initial response, I had eventually managed to negotiate one of three couches from her house, one of three beds and the vacuum cleaner. As I struggled to carry parts of the bed frame down the stairs, both Carolyn and her mum sat on the couch and continued to watch television. The set-up of the room meant that I had to cross their viewing path. This didn't instigate an offer of help from either of them but instead I was made to feel like I was intruding. When the van was loaded and I was ready to go, it was finally time to say goodbye to Carolyn. I was determined to do all the right things right up until the end. I said how sorry I was it hadn't worked between us, but her mum stepped in and just said it was a terrible failure. Carolyn and I hugged and I closed the door for the last time.

The next few hours were spent unloading the van, erecting the bed and putting the couch together. Later that day my very close network of friends had arranged a 'moving shower' for me. Plates, cups, pots and pans, towels and a tool box were just some of the items I received. My friends were amazing. It was hard not to get emotional at their kindness and generosity, and for one moment I was unable to keep my emotions internal. My sister video-called me at the height of the party. She wanted to thank my friends for their support, and this made for yet another bout of emotion from everyone.

The marriage dissolution was booked at the court for January 2017. I had wrongly assumed Carolyn would attend in full force with her family and in preparation I had two close friends with me. I was surprised to see Carolyn on her own and I actually felt a little sorry for her. The proceedings were over quickly and we were now divorced.

AS THE DAYS AND WEEKS went by, I was feeling more and more settled in my new surroundings. So it was just me and Hugo. This was the set-up I had been looking forward to for months. My transformation was amazing. Suddenly I began to thrive in all areas of my life. I was embracing work and my new single status, I had my wonderfully kind friends, I had my new home and I had Hugo all to myself again.

The geese control company for whom I worked had now given me the challenge of opening up a whole new area for them in Columbus, the capital city of the state of Ohio. As I spent more and more time in Columbus working, my friend Roberta was very kindly looking after Hugo for me while I was there. She had been the very first employee with the company and had a retired goose dog living with her. Joff and Hugo had become buddies. Their similarity in age meant they enjoyed each other's company, which besides their two daily walks was spent sleeping on the couch. April is a notoriously busy time for the company as that is when the birds are nesting. Long days were the norm during this period and with the expansion of Columbus it meant I was spending more and more time there.

Meanwhile, David, my step-dad of over 30 years, was aging rapidly. Despite his inability with modern technology we were able to video-call at least once a week. We laughed a lot on our calls, and they were such fun. I spoke to him one Saturday but we lost the connection and so on Sunday we talked for a second time. Since my move to the United States and following Mum's death I always ended the call telling him I loved him. He eventually got comfortable telling me he loved me which always made me tear up a little. He was a man of little emotion but somehow, I had managed to tap into this vulnerable side of him.

Then came my next major crisis. The following day Eve called to say David was in the hospital with a suspected heart attack. It was bad and he wasn't expected to make it through the night. I knew this day would come at some point and I prepared myself for the inevitable. I was in Columbus at the time where I had been for several days and my schedule meant I was going to be there for at least another two days. This was the first time my move to the United States was going to prove to bring a new set of emotions. Should I get a flight to London in the hope of making it in time was one of the many questions I was faced with. Eve had said I likely would not make it in time and it was more important that I would be there for the funeral. I reluctantly agreed to this and waited for the inevitable news of his passing.

The following morning, I was at a client site talking to the Maintenance Manager and I heard my phone ring in the car. I knew who it was and what the nature of the call was, but I needed to disguise my anxiety over the fact I was going to miss the call. When I was at the point I could get back into the car, I immediately called Eve and asked, "Do I need to pull over?" "Yes," she said in a very definite manner. I pulled over to the side at the back of the property and was given the news that David had passed away a few minutes before. There was the initial fear of familiarity of the feelings that would follow. I only had the death of my mother as a comparison and that was one of the most horrific experiences of my life. Eve explained that it had been a peaceful end and that she was with him up to the moment he passed away. I cried for ten minutes, but I was aware that I was at a client site and needing to leave as soon as I could gather enough composure to drive safely. I called my boss and explained what had happened, and she of course gave me the option of returning home to Cleveland but I declined. Instead, she made the two hour journey to meet me at my hotel. What a wonderful friend. This wasn't to be the only time she knew I needed her before I even knew. I carried on with the working day, trying to maintain composure and all the while being grateful that my job had come to the rescue once again when I needed comfort and distraction.

A couple of weeks later I made the journey to England to attend the funeral. It went as expected, which in this day and age I am thankful for. Despite the circumstances around my trip it was of course lovely to see my family and friends. Roberta was once again looking after Hugo for me while I was away. She explained that while out on their usual daily walk he had slipped in the wet grass and was limping. I wasn't too worried as with his weakened and arthritic hips small injuries were unfortunately not uncommon and he soon bounced back after some rest. When I returned to Ohio, I was questioning myself over the death of David and was uncomfortable with some of my decisions. Those choices were dictated by my location away from my English home, and I knew I needed to mentally work through them to relieve the guilt I felt at not being there during the final moments of his life or indeed as support for Eve in the days following. That was one of the hardest aspects. Since Mum had died, Eve and I had become much closer. We had shared a life-changing experience that only she and I had encountered. It was one that was so distressing, it was difficult to put into words.

As part of my continuing mental rehabilitation, I needed to accept my decisions in order to be comfortable with them and start to move on. I broke it down into stages: -

- The Event was the death of David.
- The Decision was not to return to England immediately. I made the decision based on the information I had at the time.

I had to accept this decision as being the right one. Once I had accepted it, I was able to have a sense of calm about the situation. This then enabled me to move on. I apply this psychological chain to many aspects of my life and it is now key to my well-being.

- Acceptance is the final link in achieving success, no matter what the circumstances, breaking down every aspect, dissecting all the possibilities and choices that were made. With the mantra, 'I made the decision based on the information I had at the time', it is pretty much foolproof. Unlike years ago, when I would respond impulsively to most situations, I now take the time to evaluate every possible outcome. Ultimately, I am minimising the chance of regrets in my decision making.

When I look back on my life up to this point, I realise that it has been something of a roller coaster. Moments of happiness punctuated by long periods of depression and anxiety. But since my move to America and my re-emergence as a responsible adult living on my own, I have begun to realise that I now have the tools to combat whatever life might throw at me. I had got through the loss of close family. I had survived a most unpleasant relationship. But now, the next momentous development was about to test me once more.

Hugo was not getting any better after his fall and so I took him to the vet. I was advised that he had torn the ACL ligament in his knee joint and would need surgery. June of 2017 is when Hugo had the operation to repair his knee. I knew he was sensitive to anaesthetic and took an unusually long time to recover. This was no exception and he spent two extra nights in the intensive care unit of the veterinary hospital. When I went to visit him, I was told the high-pitched crying was a side-effect of the pain relief he was on. To say it was distressing was an understatement. His eyes were glossy and he was panting heavily in his recovery kennel. When he was eventually allowed home, I stayed with him in the living room overnight. I was so grateful I had hung out for a ground floor apartment. There wasn't a single stair anywhere that we would have to manage during his recovery.

We both missed our walks for the next three months and instead I bought a 'Pet Stroller' which meant he could still enjoy the outside without compromising his recovery. As I pushed him along the streets, people in oncoming cars were greatly amused, especially on the days he insisted on carrying his favourite soft toy, fondly known as 'Birthday Cake!' With rest and rehabilitation, he was getting stronger every week. His rehab vet had a soft spot for Hugo and all three of us looked forward to our sessions together. He continued to make everyone who met him laugh and smile.

The summer was coming to an end and the possibility of one more day at the beach with Hugo was slowly disappearing, but one last hot day at the end of September saw us at our favourite spot on the beach of Lake Erie. He got so puppy-like when he was swimming. We had our usual routine of me throwing his water toy far out into the lake and he would enthusiastically run in to retrieve it. When he got back to the beach he would drop it in the sand and signal for me to come over to launch it again, but he would then grab it and shake it so most of the sand would fall off. When he did eventually drop it, he would bark until I threw it back into the lake for him to retrieve. It was the same routine for 20 minutes or so and we both loved it. It was our best thing to do together. This was definitely a plus of us moving to Ohio!

A MAJOR PART OF MY mental well-being is having daily quiet time. This is when I process all of the day's events and try to put them in some sort of comfortable order so they are ready to be mentally filed. It was one of these moments that inspired me to write to President Obama at the White House. Although my move from England had been because of my love for Carolyn, I found myself falling in love all over again but this time with Ohio, and it was down to the former President changing the law on DOMA (Definition of Marriage Act) that I was able to live a life with my then love, Carolyn.

I am now so content living on my own with Hugo. I have a great work/life balance and am feeling fulfilled in every aspect. At long last, I AM HAPPY. I have peace in my mind, which is what I have strived to achieve for decades.

Chapter 13

Lucky for some!

I'M NOT SUPERSTITIOUS, BUT I'M also not taking any chances!

Chapter 14

Going home for Christmas. A drama with immigration.
My worst fear comes true.

I WAS EXCITED TO BE spending Christmas 2017 with my family in England, something I hadn't been able to do since my move to the United States.

Birthdays and Christmas in particular were a difficult time when I was so far away. The time leading up to the festivities and of course with Mum's passing on Christmas Eve, was inevitably a time filled with emotional challenges. The signs of the so-called 'best time of the year' seemed to be getting earlier and earlier and it wasn't unusual to see the flickering, sparkling lights in front gardens coupled with the inflatable snowman and Santa in November! This year I was determined to embrace all that Christmas represented. I had historically struggled with the celebratory side of Christmas and was on the verge of accepting this was as good as it was going to get, most likely for the rest of my life. Seeing the lights didn't bring me joy but instead made me a little angry and of course sad.

But being around family was going to help my desire to embrace all of Christmas. I did a good job! Eve and I went to the local church on December 24th. We have never been particularly religious types, but this was one day in the year when we felt a sense of duty in lighting a candle for the people we had lost. With the passing of David in April there would be another candle added to the ceremonial lighting. This ritual confirmed the closeness that Eve and I now enjoyed. It was actually a blessing as a result of tragic circumstances. For the first year since Mum's passing I actually managed to hold it together and it became almost matter of fact. We never stayed for more than ten minutes in the church, because that was all that was required in order to achieve what we set out to do.

Christmas Day was actually full of joy. It felt different this year. Being surrounded by family was clearly what I needed, and as a consequence the day was full of laughter and tons of love. Dad and Jane had very kindly arranged temporary membership for me at *Champneys*, their private members' health club. Jogging on the treadmill next to my Dad was surprisingly rather a proud moment. There he goes again, being my inspiration!

When it came time to say our goodbyes at Heathrow there was of course that familiar heavy sinking feeling. Deep breaths were certainly what was required in order to maintain composure during the 'drop off'. It was now time to go into practical mode once more. The journey back to the U.S. was long and required two flights, the first usually being to New York although I had taken several alternative routes such as via Canada, then there was the short internal flight back to Cleveland. As I stood in the check-in line to deposit my bag, I was approached by a *United Airlines* staff member. She asked for my passport and Green Card. I explained that my Green Card had expired but I had a letter in replacement which gave me a one year extension on my Permanent Residency. I was pulled out of the line and asked to wait in a corner next to a bar in the main concourse while a United States Immigration Officer looked over my file. I wasn't worried as everything was in order. I had a pending I-751 Petition, in other words I had applied for my 10-year Green Card and it was being processed. After a 45 minute wait, the Immigration Officer approached me and asked several questions about my status and my marriage to Carolyn. She then moved 20 feet away from me and made a phone call. On her return she announced I would not be taking that flight as my paperwork was insufficient. When it comes to immigration it is very black and white, either you meet the requirements or you don't. There was no point in trying to convince her to let me fly. She escorted me to the *United Airlines* desk where they made the cancellation. The Officer said I had to go to the United States Embassy in London to get a 'Transportation Document' and because I was a permanent resident there would be no need for me to make an appointment, so if I hurried I could make a flight later that day. I made the phone call to Dad to explain what had happened and what I needed to do. Without delay I found the luggage storage facility and checked in my bags. I then used the Heathrow Express train service to go into the centre of London.

I was relying heavily on my smart phone to get me from point A to point B and after an hour I arrived at the embassy. Heavily guarded with armed police officers around all four sides of the building, it was slightly intimidating to say the least. I made my way to the security gate and explained my situation, but the guard refused me entry, saying that I needed to send an email to 'USCIS' (United States Citizenship and Immigration Services) and unless my name was on the list, there was no way I was getting access to the building. It was very much by appointment only and their appointments were held on Tuesdays and Thursdays only. Today was Thursday. Feeling extremely frustrated, I accepted that the soonest I was going to be able to get an appointment was the following Tuesday, so the next task in hand was to make sure I got the first available appointment. I used my phone to send the email while I was outside the embassy and received a reply within 5 minutes with a link to a government website which gave instructions on how to obtain the Travel Documents. Every time you complete a form for immigration purposes there is a fee and there was no exception to this one. I had to pay $645 in order to get the appointment and wait for the confirmation.

Then I had to go back to Heathrow to collect my bags and arrange for Dad to pick me up. By this time the battery on my phone was at zero and had turned itself off. So then I had to search for a charging outlet at Heathrow! This just added to the stress. Whenever I am away from Hugo, he is what makes me want to go back. I was missing him so much and having gone from being only a few hours away to now six days away was quite unbearable. When I returned to Dad's and Jane's house I immediately got on the computer and sent the required documents to the embassy, one of which was my flight confirmation. I called *United Airlines* and made a new booking for the following Wednesday, because I figured this would help my cause in getting an appointment on Tuesday. It did and the following morning I got an email confirming my midday appointment.

The next four days were a mix of frustration and sadness at not being able to return. I so needed to get back to Hugo. On the flip side I got to spend more time with my family but in the back of my mind was the question of whether I was actually going to be able to return. I got a glimpse of how I would feel if I ever had to move back to England. It wasn't a feeling I particularly liked. The grey skies and the endless rain made it difficult to want to stay, and it was all too familiar of how I had lived for years in my own head with the grey and black of depression. Home was now where my Hugo was.

The following Tuesday I made my way back to the embassy. Everything was in order and I was handed two envelopes with strict instructions not to open either of them. One was for the airline at check-in and the other for the Immigration Officer once I landed in the USA. The next day we then had to endure the painful goodbye once again at the Heathrow departure drop-off point. I was nervous of course and so desperate to get back. Check-in was accomplished without delay, and I was at last on my way home.

As we touched down in New York I made my way to the Immigration desk and handed over the second letter. The man immediately got on his radio and called for another officer to take me to where I would be escorted for secondary screening. There were about twenty people in the side room with two desks that were very high up. There was a mix of all nationalities and all ages but with one objective in common and that was to gain entry into the United States. My name was called and I approached the desk where I was again asked questions about my marriage to Carolyn and my pending Green Card application. I was then told to sit back down. The officers are quite intimidating, and you are at their mercy and they know it. Again, I was called up to the desk, a few more questions asked and again told to sit back down. The third time I was called up was the last time. He stamped my passport and told me to be on my way. The relief was enormous, I was going to be picking up Hugo from Roberta in just a few hours. Of course, my bag was no longer on the carousel and it was sitting on its own in the concourse. I checked in for my internal flight, got to the gate and headed for the bar. I ordered a shot, drank it in one go and began to make my phone calls.

Once I had arrived in Cleveland I was going to get an Uber ride home, pick up the car and immediately collect Hugo. Can you imagine my surprise and happiness that on the escalator making my way towards the exit at Cleveland Hopkins Airport I saw four of my closest friends with balloons and signs welcoming me home! I had no idea they were going to do this, but it was characteristic of the kindness I have been shown by my new friends ever since I arrived in Cleveland. I was overcome with the sense of being back where I was meant to be, so I guess that meant I was home.

When I returned, I immediately got straight back into work. Although I was able to do some work while in England for the extra days, I was conscious of the additional time I had been away and needed to make up for the unscheduled vacation.

February rapidly approached, and we were at the start of the spring season at work. It was as expected, phone calls, emails and not enough hours in the day to keep up but I was enjoying it. On Monday I was in Columbus for our bi-weekly staff meeting. That same week I was scheduled to be back in Columbus on Wednesday, so normally I would stay overnight and spend the time doing sales calls and building up the client list. Although I knew Hugo was in good hands with Roberta I was missing him terribly and wanted to return to Cleveland. I think I was still healing from the traumatic experience of not being able to return from England and I sought comfort in being in my apartment with my Hugo. My boss was quite insistent that I stay in Columbus as I was returning for another meeting no more than 36 hours later, but I simply said, "I want to return to my dogs, I miss them," and I went against their wishes and returned to Cleveland anyway. I don't know why but at the time I felt strongly about returning.

It was some years since Hugo was able to jump so lifting him on and off the bed and in and out of the car was just part of my day. An 80lb hunk of chocolate Labrador is no small task. I had shared my bed with Hugo for years and I know I slept better with him there. There was no such thing as sleeping in as 6.30am or sometimes earlier he was up and ready for breakfast, but Wednesday February 7th was different. Hugo didn't get up at 6.30 or indeed 7am. At 7.30 I lifted him off the bed and took him outside. His first pee of the morning ended the same way each time and that was with a little happy dance as if to say, "Yay, now it's time for breakfast!" He would even run a little, back into the apartment and wait with anticipation as I poured a cup of kibble into his dish. On this occasion though he just sniffed the bowl and went to lay down in his bed. The alarm bells were going off in my head that something was not right about this at all. If Hugo didn't want to eat, then it was serious.

As I looked at him he appeared almost bloated on one side, so this coupled with not eating made me schedule an appointment with the vet immediately. An hour later he ate his breakfast, slowly and with a little less enthusiasm but I was relieved at this. Later that morning we made our way to the vet and he hopped onto the scales. He was reluctant to release his 'birthday cake' toy but I was insistent when it came to a check on his weight.

I explained Hugo's symptoms and that we had been in three weeks ago because of a tick in his ear. The vet looked at his chart and said he had gained five pounds in three weeks. He took him off for an ultrasound and I nervously waited for him to return. Several minutes passed by and the vet came back into the room, saying, "I would like to show you what the ultrasound has shown us." I followed him up the hallway into a side room where Hugo was laying on the table with a nurse comforting him. As he passed the probe over his stomach he explained that there was a huge mass that had been growing for some time. Hugo didn't eat his breakfast because he was bleeding internally. It then clotted, and he felt better momentarily enabling him to feed again. My hands involuntarily began to shake, and I could tell from the look on the vet's face and the quiet tone of his voice that this was not good. They could operate to remove the mass but there was a high chance Hugo would not survive the surgery and an even higher chance of the mass re-growing. The recovery for this type of surgery is particularly long and hard. With that information I knew surgery was not an option and it was a case of when are we going to put Hugo to sleep, today, tomorrow, next week.

I needed some time to think about this and call family and friends for comfort and advice. Dad, Jane and Eve were the first calls I made. They knew a call from me like this was inevitable but not like that, it was so quick. Hugo would bleed again, we didn't know when, it could be in five minutes or five days but he would only deteriorate and one of the bleeds would be massive. I had to make the terrible decision to have Hugo put to sleep, but then I had to decide when. Many people in a similar situation choose to keep their pet alive. Clouded by the grief of their imminent demise, they do what's right for them and not what's right for the animal. I was determined not to be one of those people. I could have taken him home for one more night, but I would have wanted him for one more night after that and where would it end? It wouldn't. So with the support of my family and friends, I decided Hugo was going to end his life there and then.

Roberta and my boss Marsha were on their way to the vet to be a support for me once again. They called in on my apartment on the way and collected Hugo's teddy bear, the same one he had kept since he was eight weeks old, and also the blanket we used to snuggle with on the bitterly cold Ohio winter days. Hugo and I were in the room that I had dreaded visiting for many months. It was located close to the reception area and the sign on the door was 'special exam room'. Everyone knew what took place in there but of course never wanted to be faced with having to take their beloved pet in. I realised that this dark day would eventually come, I knew how long Labradors normally live, and so I had been preparing myself for a long time. It was imperative I made all the right decisions as I was able to imagine in the weeks following how my decisions would affect my recovery. At this critical time, with yet another personal crisis having to be faced, I had to call upon the therapy that I had been taught.

Hugo was pleased to see Marsha and Roberta, and energetically and enthusiastically greeted them as they came into the special exam room. The vet entered shortly afterwards, and the tension began to build. I was confused because Hugo seemed to be so well at that moment. Teddy in his mouth and his joyful verbalising that we had all come to love so much somehow made the final decision even harder for me to make. Eventually he laid down on the blanket and the needle was inserted into his leg. "This will send him to sleep," the vet explained, "and the second injection will stop his heart." I held Hugo tightly through the first and second injections. One final gasp for air and he was pronounced dead. I carried on holding him for ten minutes afterwards but knew I had to leave at some point. I couldn't stop looking at him. I wanted him to be engraved onto my mind so the loss wouldn't be so real. I stepped backwards towards the door, turned my back and walked slowly into the car park. The disbelief, emptiness and fear were overwhelming as we made our way to the car.

'What am I going to do now?' was the question going over and over in my mind. Roberta and Marsha both came into my apartment and I made a cup of tea for us. I had taken chicken out of the freezer that morning as it was Hugo's favourite, but what was I going to do with the chicken now? Sporadic moments of tears followed in the days proceeding. Moments of staring into nothing were frequent and an inability to concentrate was all too evident. I had to make the phone calls to friends to give them the sad news and I was surprised by some of their reactions. Tears were common, not just from the people who had known Hugo for years but grown men who had had the pleasure of knowing Hugo for no more than a year were unsuccessfully fighting the emotion.

I continued to take my daily walk, doing the exact same route we did every day but over time this has lessened, and I no longer get that initial comfort it first brought, so now I don't do it. Before Hugo's death I had a routine of going to the gym in my apartment complex early in the morning before work. I was never gone for more than an hour but when I returned we were equally excited to see each other. The pain of returning to the empty apartment after the gym then became too much and so I stopped doing that too. His bed, bowls and toys stayed in the same place for weeks and eventually one by one I would put them in a cupboard. All except for 'Birthday Cake', which is now my new sleeping buddy!

I was worried about me. Not because of how I was feeling at the time but because of how I might feel later that day or maybe tomorrow. I needed a coping plan which was 50% thought process and 50% physical. I concentrated on what I had and not what I had lost. I had to accept that Hugo was gone. I was feeling the benefit of years of preparation for this and of course my choices leading up to his death. I had made all the right decisions and again I was being psychologically rewarded for this insight.

Unlike Mum's death, there were two sides to this grief. The emotional loss and the physical loss. Hugo had been with me pretty much 24 hours a day for almost twelve years. He had helped me through two marriages, two divorces, numerous homes, jobs and a move across the ocean. For the first time since moving to America I felt lonely. Not alone, but lonely. Everyone has a story to tell about Hugo and how he constantly made them laugh. It was very apparent that he brought a lot of joy into many people's lives. Condolence cards arrived from England and the United States, including from his vet and his physical therapist whom we had come to love during his recovery from ACL surgery.

As I write this chapter four months after losing Hugo, I know I am still grieving. Every day I analyse how I am feeling, how many actions will affect my next feeling. I am very much protecting myself from my own brain because I know what it's capable of. Losing Hugo is one of the worse things that can happen to me and is a major trigger for the depression from which I am in remission. BUT I AM STRONG. I know now how to deal with this. I have had to survive so many problems in my life that I am sure I can deal with this. It will take time, and Hugo will always be with me in spirit, but I have to be positive, remember all the good things in my life, and move on.

Sammie and Hugo, together always.

C h a p t e r   1 5

What I have learned. How I have survived.

THIS IS QUITE POSSIBLY THE most important chapter in this book, because it is how I reached my current state of well-being and how it is maintained. I am not medically qualified in any way, so this is just from my own personal experience.

People comment on how laid-back I am now, how I don't take things to heart and that I am a happy and joyful person to be around! This still amazes me no end. But it is true. So how did I get to my current state of well-being and how do I maintain it especially through the inevitable low points that life throws at us?

Recovery literally took years. I had to find the right combination of drugs and therapy and I had to learn as much about my mind as possible. Observing myself in situations and knowing my triggers were key. For me, mindfulness was a key component in my recovery. Dealing with that one moment and not seeing too far ahead, as that is just too overwhelming at times. Depression thrives on assumptions. The 'what if's'! I have learned not to waste my time with those but to focus on the facts. If I am worried, I ask myself what I am worried about and much of the time it is an unnecessary worry based on a 'what if'.

There have been several different types of medications over the years and I have finally found the right combination. I have accepted the fact that I will probably be on medication for the rest of my life and for a short time this did bother me, but looking at the bigger picture here, so what if I am on meds for the rest of my life? If you are on medication for depression, you must make sure it is the right medication for you as an individual because often the drugs that work for one person don't necessarily work for another. So keep on trying until you find the right combination, as I have done.

I've mentioned this earlier, but it is pivotal in my success and that is, 'Every minute of every day the health of my brain is a priority'. Without this, I have nothing. It comes before everything else. My work is a large part of this maintenance and I am so grateful for this that I will never jeopardise or take advantage of my position. Although it is good to have, financial success is not particularly my goal. Peace of mind is my goal. I have found that this is achieved simply by having time. Time to analyse and process my thoughts and events, good or bad. I always make sure I have my daily 'quiet time'… no television, music, conversation or screens of any kind and just taking the time to explore my thoughts. I ask myself if the thoughts and events are going to help my well-being or not. I also ask myself what the end goal is and that will determine if I start the journey or not. Carolyn made contact with me recently and by text message she invited me for dinner. I asked myself if I had a goal to achieve as a result of accepting the invitation. The answer was no, so there simply was no point in accepting the invitation. I politely declined by not responding to the message!

Just occasionally work can be a bit overwhelming, but I recognise this and keep myself in check. While my desire is to climb the career ladder I am taking my time. I'm in no rush and if I am at the top of my career ladder now, I am perfectly content with where I am. Financially I am not struggling too much and live a simple yet comfortable life in my one-bedroom apartment. I won't ever be in a position to buy luxury cars or even a four-bedroom house overlooking the lake but I am not particularly materialistic like I used to be. In fact, when it comes to material possessions and 'stuff', I lean more towards simplicity. I'm not one for keeping things that don't necessarily have a use or purpose. My apartment is very minimalist. The walls are white with only four photos, there isn't a whole lot of colour and my bedroom is definitely a reflection of this with just my bed, two white night stands and one picture of Hugo on the wall. I think because I lived in mental chaos inside my own head for so long, I thrive on simplicity. The less I have, the less I have to see, process and interpret. I am matching the empty space in my home with the empty space in my brain, which makes for a sense of calm.

I continue to see my counsellor Bethany on an as-needed basis, which is typically once every three weeks. This is when I verbalise my thoughts and make sense of them. A lot of my realisations have occurred in my sessions with Bethany. Although she doesn't necessarily advise, she does inspire me.

I must admit that there have been times when I have rather lost my faith in human nature. Not only because of my own experiences but also events locally, nationally and globally. The world at times is an ugly place. Human behaviour disgusts me at times and so to counteract this I try to be the best I can possibly be. I limit time spent on social media and never express an opinion of any kind. I am saving myself from any possibility of confrontation. Kindness to myself and to others is crucial. Being kind to those who don't necessarily deserve that kind of generosity is hard to do but also necessary.

I work at not having the 'hate emotion', as it is not positive in my well-being. I don't hate people, but I can hate what they have done. I believe in forgiveness but only after time and only if the behaviour is not persistent. Actions of an individual can cause you to hate them, but it is you who experiences the feelings and emotions associated with that hate. The other person doesn't get to know how your hate for them makes you feel and besides, even if they do, they likely won't care.

Since moving to the United States, I have experienced the best and worst of humanity. I only surround myself with kind people now. If you are not kind-hearted I gently and politely let you go. The people in my life now are the kindest people I have ever met, and I hold onto them tightly. They constantly inspire me and motivate me to be the best possible version of myself I can be. So far, I am winning.

Here's another thought. Karma. I have never previously been an advocate of Karma, but it has taught me to manage my negative thoughts in a more positive way. The universe has a habit of knowing who should be rewarded and who should learn from their actions. This enables me to feel no need to retaliate for people who have hurt me. I hear all too often about people who want to slash the tyres of their ex's car or throw a brick through their window. I believe the universe will take care of it for me. One example of this is when I learned that Carolyn decided to move out of State shortly after our divorce. She was apparently looking for a new start. I have come to realise that a new start is not obtained through a change in place but through a change in mind. The year-long move to North Carolina before returning to Cleveland was yet another disaster for Carolyn, with another failed relationship, six months on crutches due to a torn ACL (that same injury as Hugo) and no job.

I was no part of any of this, so Karma did the work. I just had to sit back and feel sorry for her as her striving for a new start didn't get off the ground because she didn't have a change in mind. Always chasing something to grab a hold of in the hope it will make life better doesn't work. You can chase for years and years looking for that new start that will bring a happier and more fulfilled life, but without internal mental growth and acceptance there is no new start.

A typical response when you announce you are in a new relationship is a question… 'does she make you happy?' 'Well, yes,' is the expected reply. All too often we are chasing happiness and expecting other people to bring it to us in a relationship. When it falls short of expectation the relationship will eventually end and you are left with disappointment. We rely too heavily on others making us happy and not ourselves. Unlike years ago, I now don't rely on someone else to make me happy. I am already happy. Being with someone you have feelings for may bring that out further, but it is by no means the sole reason for my happiness. Should the relationship end, I won't lose everything, I will just lose a little.

A word about Self Esteem. I am constantly challenging myself. It can be small stuff like leaving the dishes in the sink overnight and not clearing them away until the following day. Being a neat freak, cleanliness and order is something I thrive on. When I see the dirty dishes the following morning, there is that initial discomfort that comes with my decision to leave them there but ultimately, I pat myself on the back. I lived for many years knowing exactly what I would be doing at what time, where I would be, always turning up to a meeting on time or a few minutes early, I certainly never lost anything as everything had its place. Things are different now. I occasionally lose my keys or my phone and I am even sometimes a few minutes late for a meeting and I love it! I am now at last in control of me.

If I succeed in my 'mini challenges', I get to feel good about myself with a sense of accomplishment and that increases my self-esteem. If I don't complete the challenge (note I don't use the word fail) then as long as I learn from not succeeding and I can apply it next time, I am using the experience positively. There is so much pressure to be number one, to be the best and to win but success is not measured by the end result, rather by the effort.

An example of this is a recent challenge I set myself and that was to lose 50lbs in 12 months. I had three months left and I realised that I was unlikely to succeed. I hadn't given up, but the expectation was that I would not lose 50lbs in 12 months. If I am not successful in completing the challenge, that will lead to another challenge and that is how to deal with apparent failure. I can dwell on the fact I didn't lose 50lbs and that will affect my self-esteem, or I can embrace the fact and be okay with it, that in itself is the challenge. When and if the time comes, I will choose the latter of the two options. I will have tried my best. Success is measured by effort, remember, and not by the end result.

Cognitive Behavioural Therapy, or CBT as it is commonly known, is also paramount. Glass half full and all that! I apply it to most things, and here's an example.

A friend of mine never wears his seat belt. He has a job that involves a lot of driving and is constantly in and out of the car. He got pulled over by Highway Patrol and was slapped with a $150 ticket. When he called me, he was angry at himself, not for failing to wear his seat belt, but for getting the financial penalty. He lives within a budget and this is a big hit on his income. His anxiety was high, and he was mad. After he had calmed down, I asked him if he was going to wear his seat belt from now on and to my surprise, he said no. For whatever reason and it may be simple stubbornness, he isn't going to change his behaviour. I thought about this for a minute and said to him, "How about you wear your seat belt, not for the sake of wearing your seat belt, but to save you from feeling the way you currently do again when you inevitably get another ticket?" He took a few moments and then said, yes. He is changing the reason for wearing it which ultimately makes him do the right thing and removes any possibility of another $150 fine. A few days later I called him and asked if he was wearing his seat belt. He replied, "Hell, yeah." Job done!

After years of self-evaluation, I have eventually found out my seven stages to happiness. They are: Experience, Thought, Emotion, Feeling, Acceptance, Opportunity, Healing.

One of life's most stressful events is divorce, so I would like to apply this theory to this scenario.

The Experience is my wife has left me. The Thoughts are, "I will be on my own, how will I support myself financially, who will look after me, how will I fill my day, with whom am I going to share my life, it's me and I'm not good enough anymore?"

Then come the Emotions… abandonment, worry, loneliness. All of these are a result of the thought, none of which are guaranteed. I ask myself for evidence and inevitably there isn't any.

The Feelings then start to hit and they can be physical, emotional or both.

Nausea, racing heart rate, the feeling of being paralysed, body aches, headaches, dizziness. The body can't sustain this level of anxiety (flight or fight) indefinitely which is when the mind takes over and depression sets in. This is when the cycle needs to be interrupted.

Acceptance is when you realise you can't change the past and don't dwell on the things you cannot change. 'You made the decision based on the information you had at the time', so this enables you to be comfortable with the decision. Having evaluated all the options available to you, dissecting them and seeing how they will affect you and others with the least amount of collateral damage, then *knowing* you made the right choice in the end. A key part of acceptance is the ability to mentally revisit the event without the traumatic thoughts and feelings that previously surrounded it.

Opportunity – my wife can no longer live with me. It's a fact but also a negative, so I turn the initial thoughts into opportunities. 'How will I support myself?' I can get a new career or progress in my current job.

'Who will look after me?' I will look after me. My mental well-being and insight into myself will enable me to thrive.

'How will I fill my day?' New interests and priorities and a gradual sense of calm along with contentment will fill my day.

'I'm no longer good enough.' That is a direct, non-evidence based thought. If your spouse tells you that you are no longer good enough, that is a feeling that they have, they own it, not you. Don't accept it, it's not yours to have. Don't allow this thought to go into an emotion.

'Who am I going to share my life with?' I will share my life with me, and having lived for so long not having myself I will realise that is enough.

I try to see an opportunity in everything. Even when Hugo passed away I was focusing on what opportunities would be available to me. Travel and generally more freedom are the obvious ones but are also really big ones and I plan on taking full advantage of these opportunities. I now see the end of something as the start of something else. Every end leads to a beginning which brings new opportunities.

One example of this is through a friend of mine. Her sister has battled for many years with class A drug addiction. The grand finale is when just a few weeks ago she sold drugs to another user and the lady she sold to died as a result of an overdose. My friend's sister is now waiting on a court date where she will face a long prison sentence. My friend has confided in me on the journey which the whole family have and continue to be on. Naturally the family are in total despair at the inevitability of her prison sentence. Everyone has lost hope as this really is rock bottom. When she is eventually released she will only be able to get minimum wage jobs which do not pay enough to live independently and so the future does not look so good either.

As my friend was telling me this, I searched for any opportunity. With time in prison she will have access to education. I suggested that she could perhaps train and get qualified in counselling and when she is released there would be no person better equipped than her to help people with addiction issues. Her earning potential would be as much as a 5 or even 6 figure salary, not to mention her personal growth, self-esteem and confidence in helping other people. My friend has told me that her sister and her family now have something solid to focus on. This is a real opportunity for her to be a success and to be the best possible version of herself. It has given them all hope and made them realise the long prison sentence isn't the end, and perhaps it is the beginning and the first step towards leading a productive life on the outside.

Healing – Once the previous steps have been completed, you have the ability to be able to use your experience in a positive way, recalling once painful memories and using the experience positively. That is when life is calm, I am content, that is what I am and I'm sure millions of other people are striving for. Yes... I can say with confidence that I have finally defeated depression.

I defeated depression.

RICHARD'S STORY

PART 2

Richard's Foreword

THIS IS A BOOK I thought I would never want to write. But now that time has to a certain extent allowed me and my wife to come to terms with what happened to Sammie, my younger daughter by my first wife Tina, I have actually found it somewhat therapeutic as I know Sammie has.

Actually Sammie must take much of the credit for the idea of this book, because it was she who, when we were talking about her depression one day, came up with what seemed to my wife and me like a most surprising thought that she would like to write the story of her illness and her amazing recovery, in the hope that it would be of value to others who are going through something similar..

We are of course aware that there have been many books written by and about sufferers of clinical depression, but it was then that I had an interesting idea which I thought might make this book somewhat different from the others. During my business career I have made many hundreds of presentations and had to perform similar speaking engagements to audiences from one to over one thousand! So I was quite familiar with the need to write scripts. I had also, on behalf of my company, written and published a wide variety of pieces for trade journals. And in the latter stages of my career, I became the go-to person for both factual and 'think pieces' to appear on the company website. So, fortified by my A-Levels in English and Latin, I can turn a phrase when I need to!

I thought that if Sammie could manage to record her thoughts and feelings about the big issues in her life, which started with the realisation that she was gay, I could then respond with my and my wife's emotions and reactions to the traumatic experience of living through Sammie's long anxiety and clinical depression illness. So that is how we have written this book. Sammie wrote it chapter by chapter, which she then emailed over to me. I then wrote my and my wife Jane's reactions to the events she had described. Some of the story has not been easy to commit to paper, but once we had agreed to undertake this, it simply had to be done. And the good news, especially for those who have been or are currently affected by this insidious illness (for that is what it clearly is) is that there is light at the end of the long and very dark tunnel.

Now in her forties, Sammie has come through her illness and is now once again the happy-go-lucky person that Jane and I knew as a child. To protect our family, friends and some others mentioned, names have been changed but that apart, every single word we have written is true.

There is one more thing to be said before you read my story. And that is for me to record my love and admiration for my wife Jane, and to publicly thank her for the unstinting love and support she has given to her step-daughter Sammie throughout the years, and indeed continues to do. I have to sometimes remind myself that Sammie is not actually her birth child, and as you have already discovered, Sammie has grown to love her deeply, and I know will be forever grateful to the woman who has taken on the mantle of substitute mum to my daughter, for which I am so very grateful. And that, coupled with Sammie's continuing recovery, makes me realise that I am a very lucky man.

RICHARD'S STORY

Chapter 1

Tina's new life gives us unforeseen challenges.

LIFE IS OF COURSE A lottery. Some people say you make your own luck, others that it's all preordained. But what is certain is that it's also filled with wonderful moments, like your first kiss, marriage and the birth of your children. It's also going to produce some pretty awful moments too.

Apart from the relatively early death of my parents, there has been one really horrible moment in my life. That was when my younger daughter Sammie became mentally ill and was eventually diagnosed with clinical depression.

I've often wondered how much of an effect my divorce had on the girls, but looking back, all three of our lovely children survived, and have made happy lives for themselves. That's my two daughters and my step-son. Sammie was always a bit of a tomboy, but the photographs of her early years give no indication of what was to come. She was a sweet if somewhat mischievous child, but loving and great fun to be with. Of the two girls, I can recall that for the first few years Sammie was actually the easier child, not so prone to middle of the night traumas as her elder sister Eve. Later on, it was Eve who became the angelic child, whilst Sammie was a bit of a monkey!

Unfortunately, their mother did not take to motherhood with any enthusiasm, and struggled with even the simplest of maternal chores, so when they were both babies the night-time feeds were something with which I rapidly became familiar. I knew early on in our marriage that I had made a terrible mistake. I had actually previously ended our relationship, but she won the war of attrition and persuaded me to resume our living together. I think I just came to the conclusion that life was never perfect and that marriage, like most things, could be expected to be a compromise. I decided that I should stick it out, but that was before I met Jane.

By this time with two young children we needed a bigger house, so we bought a detached property with a nice garden in the village of Seer Green, near Beaconsfield in Buckinghamshire. And it was there that I met my future wife. As I have said, the separation from Tina was heartbreaking but necessary. Leaving my girls was devastating, but I managed to arrange regular weekend visits to our small rented house about 25 minutes away. I continued to support Tina and the girls financially but knew that I had to build a new life. So to try and help her recover from our separation, I paid for Tina to have a summer holiday in Spain. It also gave us an opportunity to have the girls for a whole fortnight rather than the occasional weekend as had been the case up to then.

After that trip our lives changed in a way that I had not anticipated. Tina had met a kind man who was also on his own, and although he lived in the north of England, he started making regular trips down south at the weekend. So the girls became more of a regular fixture with Jane and me whilst their romance blossomed. I can't help feeling that Tina could not cope with life on her own and simply made a beeline for the first available male. Although it was something of a shock when she announced that David had asked her to marry him and that she and the girls would be moving to live near Stockport, 180 miles away in the north of England. Suddenly I realised that my ability to keep contact with my girls was being put at risk. But I contented myself that I was actually rather lucky because having holidayed in southern Spain she might easily have fallen for an Arab and been carted off to Saudi Arabia!

Once again, my poor little girls' lives were being disrupted. A new, much smaller house, not in the best area, and a new school with schoolmates who must have seemed to them to speak a different language. And of course, with their southern English accents, I can only imagine the teasing that they must have had to endure in those first few months.

Luckily David accepted the principle of me seeing the girls every few weeks, so every few weeks on a Friday I would drive the 35 miles to work in London, park the car at Euston station then leave the office at around 4pm, take the fast train to Stockport, walk over the railway bridge to the other platform, meet the girls whom David and Tina had driven to the station, then take the fast train back to Euston and drive the 35 miles home with two rather weary little girls. Saturdays and Sundays were spent having fun together, then at around 4o'clock on the Sunday it was into the car, drive the 170 miles to an agreed meeting place near their home, kiss the girls goodbye and belt down the motorway to arrive home at about 11 o'clock and go straight to bed ready for the week ahead. I confess that on many occasions I had to wipe the tears from my eyes on leaving them so that I could keep the car on the road. I did that for about eight years because I was determined not to lose touch with them, and it enabled Jane and me to create a parallel family for the girls which, because of her wonderfully generous-hearted spirit, meant the girls were regularly together with their dad, step-mum and step-brother Daniel, a real family unit.

Perhaps the earliest indication of Sammie's sexuality issues was actually at the wedding reception that Jane and I held in the garden of our rented home in the beautiful Buckinghamshire village of Cholesbury after three happy years together. Throughout the civil ceremony, Eve and Sammie, accompanied by my step-son Daniel, had looked and behaved like little angels. The girls were dressed in pretty outfits with matching hats, and Dan was equally smart in page boy-style attire. All three were constantly admired by friends and family throughout the day, but halfway through the afternoon reception Sammie suddenly disappeared upstairs, to reappear having discarded her beautiful dress and wearing her favourite one-piece trouser suit-style garment. It was at least pink! She then proceeded to ride her little bicycle around the garden at high speed for the rest of the day, clearly feeling much more at home in this somewhat boyish attire. Dan and his cousin Jonathan's day was also made memorable by their self-induced introduction to alcohol by swigging the dregs from the used glasses in the kitchen! Thankfully they were discovered before any damage had been inflicted on their little livers. So, at the age of 6, Sammie had unconsciously displayed the first tendencies to lean towards male rather than female dress style and activities. We thought nothing of it at the time but perhaps it was an early indication of what was to follow.

I managed to send the girls to separate private schools and both seemed to be doing well. Early exam results were good and there was a sense that our lives were settling into a pattern in which the girls had adapted to their new environment and could also regularly enjoy family time with Jane and me. It was not just the weekends either. Tina and David found that Florida was the ideal holiday venue for them. Tina enjoyed lying in the sun and David was passionate about golf, so that meant we could have the girls whilst they were away and take our own holidays together as our family unit.

By this time my company, a marketing communications agency named

Triangle after its three founding partners, was beginning to prosper, so the partners decided to build a holiday home on the island of Menorca, to be enjoyed both by the directors and the staff. It was all planned and designed on the back of an envelope in a Menorcan bar, and amazingly was built on time and to budget!

We have wonderful memories of the three children's first flights, the first time in a foreign country, the first attempt at food that was somewhat more exotic than their English fare, and our first time as a true family on holiday together. I am especially proud of having helped to teach all three of them to swim in the pool at Villa Triangulo! So whilst I missed them during the weeks apart, I had at least managed to maintain regular contact with the girls and they seemed accepting of the routine and increasingly at ease in our environment down south. Little did we know what was to come just around the corner.

Chapter 2

Life's new routine, the shock of the first suicide attempt, Sammie gets a job.

LIFE HAD SETTLED INTO A new routine. I had to accept that because of my decision to walk away from my first marriage and Tina's decision to rapidly remarry, my girls were now 180 miles away from Jane and me. I worried that the girls would be emotionally damaged by my separation from them. They had been taken to a strange part of the country. They had had to enrol in new schools before it was obligatory to do so. They were now living in a strange house with a new step-father and a step-brother. And, I have no doubt, they were being subjected to verbal and emotional abuse simply because of the way they spoke. I made a pledge to myself that I would do whatever it took to remain in close contact with them, and with my wonderful wife's support, we started to do that. At the same time, I was working long hours helping to build an increasingly successful business whilst trying to factor in a girls' weekend every few weeks. It was not easy, and the emotional stress of saying goodbye to them on the Sunday evening after their weekend visits was overwhelming. But I knew I had done the right thing for me and for them, and I fervently hoped that one day when the girls were older, they would be able to understand why I had to leave their mum. I had just made a terrible mistake in marrying her. We were from completely different backgrounds which didn't help, and Tina's inability to cope with motherhood and clearly her lack of empathy with her children, had contributed to my decision to leave. I just could not face the thought of spending the rest of my life with her. But I remember telling both girls that whilst I had left their mum and would support her financially, in my mind I had NOT left my precious daughters and would do everything possible to stay as close to them as I could.

When the girls came down for weekends with us, I think in retrospect we all had to make such an effort to avoid any unpleasantness that we completely missed the turmoil that poor Sammie was going through. So, when I had a telephone call from *Normanton* school requesting a meeting with me, I thought it was just to discuss her future academic direction. She had never mentioned the bullying she was suffering, so it was a massive shock to be told that it was so bad they had had to suspend her from the school. The head teacher and his colleagues offered no solution to the problem, and it almost seemed as if they just wished Sammie wasn't there. However, there was one teacher who had taken a liking to her, perhaps recognising that whilst she was different from the other girls in one aspect, she was just as bright and therefore had just as much potential to develop academically. She and I spoke several times on the telephone, and she visited Sammie at home to try and help her catch up with the curriculum that she had missed. This could not have come at a worse time, because it was shortly before she was due to sit her GCSE's, and as a result of the missed lessons and the emotional stress she had been put under by some very cruel and unkind little girls, she did not attain the grades she was capable of. We learned later that she was diagnosed with ADD, Attention Deficit Disorder, the symptoms of which I sometimes recognise in myself these days, although that may just be a function of my increasing years! She had always been a bright, bubbly and enthusiastic girl who tried her best academically and who loved sport and had a natural talent for ball games. At least I had passed on something to her!

I found it very difficult to talk to her mum about the situation, and I suppose she must have felt the same. Not for the first time, it was her step-mum Jane who provided advice and support. We agreed that the best thing for Sammie was to come and live with us. Her elder sister Eve had already made that break and was enjoying life at university in London. But knowing Tina as I did, I was fearful that the loss of her other daughter might provoke another bout of the emotional instability that had dogged her for as long as I had known her. Having hurt her once, I didn't want to do it again.

So Sammie enrolled in a college near her home in the north, and for a time this was at least a major improvement in her life compared with the *Normanton* school experience. I have to say that my meeting with the principals of that establishment did not fill me with confidence that they knew how to cope with the situation. Perhaps because they had only just admitted girls to the school, they were simply unable to cope with a pupil who had admitted to being gay. Perhaps there was even an element of prejudice in the teaching staff. This was, after all, at a time when same sex relationships were regarded as something of a perversion, especially perhaps in a small town rather than in the more socially advanced conurbations.

Then came a terrifying phone call. It was Sammie telling us that she could not cope any more, and had tried to take her own life. She had swallowed a bunch of painkillers but had then panicked when she realised how she had put her life in danger. She explained that she couldn't tell her mother or her step-father David because they just wouldn't understand, so she had gone to a public phone box in the village and called us. It was a dreadful shock, but it also made us realise how much she depended on us.

We told her that she should go home immediately and go to bed. We then phoned Tina and explained what had happened. We got her doctor's name and called the surgery after-hours service. They asked how many tablets she had swallowed and once we had established that it was not life threatening, we were able to speak again to Tina and tell her not to worry. But worry we of course did. It was something that was so alien to our relatively normal, stable lifestyle that we were in shock for several days afterwards. We realised that Sammie was in turmoil over both the bullying she had suffered and because of the realisation of her sexual preference. It was time to take action.

Eventually I managed to broach the subject with Tina of Sammie moving to live with us. It is perhaps an indication of her attitude to motherhood that there was little resistance to the idea. And so, Sammie came to live with Jane and me. At last, we were a true family again.

Chapter 3

VH1 and Genesis, more suicide attempts, the horrors of the clinic,
transfer to the NHS.

SAMMIE CELEBRATED HER GRADUATION WITH the obligatory proud photo of her in mortarboard and gown, grinning like a Cheshire cat! She had always been conscious of her sister's and step-brother's academic achievements, so it must have been very satisfying for her to achieve a further education qualification. It made us wonder what might have been possible if the teaching staff at *Normanton* had got a grip of the situation earlier and had helped her achieve her full academic potential.

Our life now settled into a new phase, with Sammie working in media in London and showing real enthusiasm for life. She had always shared my love of music and had taken up playing the drums. Luckily the location of our cottage was such that the nearest neighbours were far enough away for us not to worry about complaints! I vividly remember when, during her time at the *VH1* music channel, she was invited to a filming session of one of our favourite bands, *Genesis*, in rehearsal. It was shortly after *Phil Collins* had left and they were rehearsing with a new lead singer. Sammie watched from the sidelines, and was then gobsmacked to be invited to sit in on the drums for a brief jam session! She came home that night happier than we had ever seen her.

Sammie settled into her new lifestyle, and it was not long before she started a friendship with a lady she met in the pub opposite our house. Barbara had a house in Tring just four miles away, and as with most things with our little girl, it was a full-on one hundred percent relationship from the outset. I have since learned that for people with her medical diagnosis, life is almost always an all or nothing thing. So we weren't surprised when she announced that she was going to move in with Barbara. At first everything seemed fine, but a number of decisions were made that started to put pressure on them both. Barbara had a well-paid job at the time, but was evidently unhappy with the quite pressurised lifestyle of a targeted sales person and not long after they got together, she resigned. I have wondered if her sexuality also provoked unpleasantness for her at work, because it must have been a big decision to give up a well-paid position with seemingly good prospects. But give it up she did, so it was not long before the pressure to pay the bills began to have an impact. To make matters worse, Sammie found that she could not cope with life in the fast-moving and somewhat shallow world of media and entertainment which she had been working in, and she soon found herself out of work too.

Barbara found employment in the traffic department of the local police, running a team of people monitoring the traffic cameras in the area. It was at least a reasonably secure job, if not particularly exciting or well-paid. However, I do recall her telling us that the nefarious activities of some local residents caught on camera on Friday and Saturday nights would have made a pretty good subject for the porno film industry!

Neither Barbara nor Sammie were good with money or budgeting, and started to build up debts which they were not able to service. We had to help them out financially on several occasions, although when this was designated as a loan rather than a gift, they always managed to pay us back eventually. I recall the purchase of drum kits, many household items and even a motorbike contributing to their declining financial security. This was I believe in part due to them seeing the lifestyle enjoyed by Sammie's sister and step-brother, both of whom were forging successful careers, which I think Sammie found frustrating compared with her own situation.

Eventually, however, Sammie and Barbara realised that they could no longer make ends meet, and so they moved to a small house on a new estate in Leighton Buzzard, half an hour away from the rather more salubrious area of the Chilterns. It was a new-build three-bedroom house on a big estate which combined both private properties and some social housing. At this point they acquired a new member of the family in the shape of a lovely chocolate Labrador named Hugo, or to give him his full adopted name, Hugo Brown! Little did we imagine just how much of an influence that animal would have on Sammie, and indeed how crucial he would become in her eventual recovery from anxiety and depression. It's well known now that animals have genuinely therapeutic qualities that can be of great help to people with mental health conditions, and this was never more so than with Hugo and Sammie.

The three of them, Barbara, Sammie and Hugo, settled in, but again the spending bug was causing problems. Just how big a problem we didn't know until they asked again for our help. When we discovered the extent of their profligacy, we were shocked and very angry. Between them they had managed to run up massive credit card debts, an appalling situation which was irresponsible to say the least. Once again it was the bank of Dad and Jane to the rescue, which allowed them to continue living in the new house provided Sammie could find employment. However, her experience in the London offices had left her with an inferiority complex, caused in no small measure by the kind of sexist attitudes and behaviour which today would be regarded as socially unacceptable. She confessed that she simply could not cope with an office environment, so was left with the uninviting prospect of working in a garage or a supermarket. Life for her had really reached rock bottom. No job, no money and increasing pressure on her relationship as a result.

By this time Sammie was beginning to exhibit symptoms of depression which we put down to her current circumstances but as it turned out, things were to become far more serious. Barbara took her to see their GP, and after questioning her at length, the doctor referred her to a psychiatrist so that she could be professionally assessed. Jane accompanied her on this visit, and when it transpired that she was actively contemplating suicide it was recommended that she immediately become an in-patient at a leading private medical clinic which specialised in mental health problems.

The shock of being told that my younger daughter was mentally ill and needed psychiatric care in a clinic was unexpected and unimaginable. I suppose I thought that this sort of thing just didn't happen to 'normal' people like us, but we were soon to discover just how unwell Sammie had become. We drove her to a private clinic in Harrow-on-the-Hill on the outskirts of London, and passing the famous Harrow boys' school only emphasised how desperate her condition had become. There were the sons of the wealthiest and most powerful people in the land, and here we were, en route to a mental health clinic just around the corner. As it turned out, the only similarity was in the size of the fees both these institutions charge!

We arrived at 12.30pm and were ushered into the communal dining room for lunch. We sat at a table with some of the patients, and consumed our meal almost in silence. Sammie spent most of that meal weeping, which was most distressing for us. After lunch we had a brief discussion with her psychiatrist who explained that she would be treated with a combination of drugs to control her emotions and CBT, cognitive behavioural therapy, to provide her with methods of dealing with her negative feelings. Even at that stage I don't think we realised the extent of her depression, and that she really was at risk of committing suicide.

Soon it was time for us to leave. We said goodbye in her small single room and left her almost hysterical, with a look of misery and terror on her face that I will never forget. We walked back to the car, but it was just too much for me and I burst into tears. Jane, equally upset, tried to comfort me but it was the beginning of a 3-month nightmare that was to become emotionally draining and as it turned out, financially crippling. At the time she had private medical insurance from her employers, but after three weeks her financial limit had been reached and so it was down to us to foot the weekly bills.

We visited Sammie several times a week for the three months that she was in the clinic. Communication was difficult because of her heavy medication, and no matter how hard we tried to encourage her to reassess her life, there seemed to be very little improvement. Barbara and Sammie's elder sister Eve would also visit her, and I know how equally difficult they found it. Looking back, I realise that she was on the heaviest dose of medication. We would arrive and be escorted to her room. There was always an atmosphere of immense sadness about the whole place, and one got the impression that whilst the staff were very caring, there was not much success to report for the inmates. We would find Sammie either still in bed or sitting disconsolately on the edge of her bed, staring into space. She would hardly acknowledge us, and would have little to offer in the way of conversation. Let's face it, when you are feeling at rock bottom what is there to say? We would chat about everyday things that had happened to us, but it all seemed so inconsequential in the face of the magnitude of Sammie's condition.

If we were lucky and he was in between consultations, we would grab a few minutes with her consultant. He explained that she was, in his opinion, very unwell and needed constant care and supervision because they were concerned about her mental state. Basically, they felt that she was a suicide risk, which was extremely upsetting to hear, even though we were by now used to this kind of conversation. We were told about the treatment she was receiving, which seemed to us that she would be drugged up to the eyeballs but was expected to participate in talking sessions along with other patients. We also noticed that her weight was ballooning because of the medication and three meals a day routine, which let's face it, was the only thing she had to look forward to. In fact, the only positive thing about our visits was the occasional slice of carrot cake baked by the lovely chef at teatimes!

On one occasion we were informed that Sammie's condition had deteriorated. There was evidence of self-harming and we were told that she had been put on 24-hour one-to-one watch. What I was not told was that this would result in an increase in the weekly fees. We started to wonder if the treatment she was receiving was appropriate, because there was little or no evidence of any improvement in her mental state. There was certainly no organised exercise, something that these days would be seen as a useful and necessary addition to the formal clinical treatments.

If you have never had personal contact with a member of your family who is suffering from clinical depression, you probably have little idea of just what it entails. But put simply, it is invasive and all-consuming, both for the patient and for their immediate family. Sammie seemed to us to be buried in a pit of her own making, and as hard as we tried not to, there were times when we just wanted to shake her and tell her to snap out of it. This of course is the worst possible thing you can say to a depressive, because quite simply they can't, and we never fell into that trap. They are living in the pit and no matter how hard they try and how much they want to escape, for them the only escape is to end their life. So it came as no surprise to learn from the clinic that Sammie had made attempts at ending it all, and on one occasion had absconded before being found and returned to the clinic.

Those three months were certainly one of the most distressing periods I can remember. Although Sammie's health and her path towards recovery were absolutely paramount, there was also the practical matter of the cost of staying at the clinic. I remember one day looking at my bank statements and bills, and experiencing a moment of panic because the outgoings were beginning to have a material effect on our own lives. Sammie had private medical insurance provided by her employer, but the limit was quickly reached and then it was down to us. In three months we had paid thousands of pounds in fees and medication charges, and frankly, it seemed to us that we had little to show for it. I booked a meeting with her consultant, who was sympathetic but noncommittal about her prognosis. There was nothing for it but to inform him that we simply could not continue with their level of fees and that we needed to get Sammie transferred from the private system into the NHS immediately. He understood our situation and promised to put this procedure in motion. What he didn't tell us was how long it would be before a bed could be found for her in a hospital within reasonable driving distance of her and our homes. After considerable pressure having to be exerted on the clinic, Sammie was eventually found a bed in a National Health hospital just 20 minutes from her home and half an hour from ours. We explained the practical considerations to her, and heaved a massive sigh of relief when she understood and agreed to be moved. But it soon became apparent that this seemingly positive development would be extremely short-lived.

Chapter 4

Our new home, the rental experience, One Flew Over the Cuckoo's Nest, cancelled trips, carbon monoxide poisoning, a way forward.

AT ABOUT THIS TIME WE had sold our lovely Chilterns cottage and purchased a barn that was in the process of being converted into a contemporary dwelling. Jane and I are sun lovers and we had always wanted a house with a beautiful south-facing garden. Jane was the first to spot the builder's sign down a lane about a mile and a half from where we were living. She came back excited, so we decided to make contact. We were lucky because they had not yet formally put it on the market, and summoning up all my powers of salesmanship, I managed to persuade them to sell us the property even without paying a deposit. The only problem was that their timescales turned out to be very different to their original estimate of completion, and because they had also agreed to let us alter the internal design, I didn't feel able to insist on a late completion penalty clause. Our cottage sold locally within days of going on the market, so there was no option other than to look for rented accommodation in the area, for as we had been led to believe, about three months. We were lucky to find a small development of refurbished properties in the next village, and so we put most of our belongings into storage and settled into our new temporary home. In fact, one of the other cottages was occupied by *Rick Wakeman* of the progressive rock group *YES*, but he turned out to be somewhat reclusive and refused my invitation to Xmas drinks. By the way, I'm still a fan!

Sammie came on a pass-out from the clinic but the visit was a disaster and really quite unsettling for all of us. On the first morning Jane brought her a cup of tea in bed, but was dismayed to discover her weeping and trembling under the bedclothes. She was clearly going through some sort of crisis, claiming that she could see death in the woods a few hundred yards away and was being told to go there to meet it. There was nothing for it but to persuade her to return to the clinic again, a decision she was only too ready to accept because it meant she would be far away from the trauma of actually visualising death as it had appeared to her.

I am a pretty normal, rational person although I can get quite emotional, and at this time I have to admit that our life seemed to me to be at its lowest ebb. Completion of the new house was constantly delayed, I was under massive stress at work with an impossibly difficult business partner, and now my younger daughter seemed to us to be closer to suicide than ever before. We both felt so helpless, not knowing how to help our poor little girl.

On another occasion, we took her to see our new home which was in the course of being refurbished and rebuilt. It had originally been a hay barn and pony stables and had been used as part of the Riding for The Disabled premises. The original oak frame had been retained and a new frame had also been added. Sammie took one look at the beams and announced that this would be an ideal place for her to tie a rope around so that she could end her life. We just felt so desperate, not knowing how to stop what seemed an inevitable rush towards the unthinkable ending.

Eventually, however, a bed became available in the mental health ward at Luton General Hospital, about 20 minutes away from her home in Leighton Buzzard. So, with a heavy heart I settled the final account at the clinic and drove her to the hospital. The scene at Luton was like an episode of *One Flew Over the Cuckoo's Nest* but without any of the humour. The staff were clearly overwhelmed and there was little evidence of any consultants on the ward. Leaving Sammie there was even worse than our first departure from the private clinic.

It was no surprise then that after just one night she was on the phone, again weeping uncontrollably and begging me to get her out of there. But this was not as easy as it seemed. The patient has to be professionally assessed and passed as not a danger to themselves or anyone else. I had to tell Sammie that unless she could convince the authorities that she was fit to leave, she would be confined to that ward for an indefinite period. The combination of some tough talking, together with the realisation that at the end of the day it was only she herself who could do this, had the desired effect. She was given a weekend pass, and was so relieved to be out of the hospital that I think she began for the first time to resolve to deal with her condition herself in the future. After further short passes and assessments, she and I attended an assessment meeting with about fifteen people. At the hospital. It must have gone well because she was signed off as an in-patient and formally transferred to the Leighton Buzzard mental health authorities. So she was back home, and back to life with a partner whose patience had been tested to the limit. To be fair to Barbara, she had shouldered much of the stress of living with an anxiety prone depressive, and was clearly at the end of her tether.

Some time later we decided to take the whole family away for the weekend as an antidote to the stress we were all feeling. I guess it must have been a special birthday but I don't recall the details. We also felt it would be part of Sammie's rehabilitation to enjoy a weekend away with the family. I found a small privately-owned castle in the Cairngorms in a beautiful part of Scotland, an area of the UK that none of us had been to before, so this was booked for two nights and the flights for all twelve of us from Heathrow to Scotland arranged.

We knew Sammie was excited by the idea but also a little nervous. However, we were not prepared for the telephone call the day before departure, telling us that she simply couldn't face the trip. She had also developed a fear of flying, yet another challenge for her and us to cope with. We tried our best to change her mind but she wasn't having it. She suggested that we should all go without her, but to my mind that defeated the object of the trip, a get-together which would include everyone in the family. With a heavy heart I rang the castle owners and told them the reason we had to cancel. They were very sympathetic and refunded part of the cost but of course we lost the flights too.

Sammie, Jane and I decided that we had to tackle the fear of flying issue, because if she could not conquer it her life would be so much less fulfilling. I researched the opportunities, and with the family's help we enrolled her in the *British Airways* course for people with a paranoid fear of air travel. Amazingly it worked, and as her future life turned out, this was one of the best things we have ever done for her.

Sammie found a job with a new small I.T. company in Tring, where she became the office manager. Since the owner was always out and about, she was left pretty much to her own devices, and it was interesting to us that she had sufficient personal discipline that she was quite happy to field phone calls, do the books and keep the place running smoothly by herself in the office. She was proud of herself for having found employment and she introduced me to the owner, Colin. At the time my own career was coming towards its final phase and I thought it would be interesting to help Colin develop his business acumen. He was keen, enthusiastic and hard-working but lacked any formal business training. It seemed the ideal opportunity for me to test my mentoring skills. He had no financial expertise so I offered to introduce him to my company's accountant who had looked after us professionally and personally for many years. I drove Colin up to London and we met James for lunch near his West End offices. The meeting was not a success. Colin was clearly out of his depth and I think was nervous about making any kind of commitment either to James or me. Yet he still wanted to find an outside investor to help him grow the business. James called me the next day to suggest I took the conversation no further. I immediately agreed and curtailed any further discussions with Colin.

The premises where Colin and Sammie worked were pretty basic by modern office standards, being converted light industrial in style. And then a strange thing happened. Sammie started to complain of constant headaches, which became so bad that she would often have to leave work early. At first, she had no idea why this was happening, and to be frank we just put it down to the never-ending saga of bad luck which had dogged her all her life to date.

On her mum's and step-dad's next visit to her sister Eve, Sammie took David round to the office on the Saturday morning when Colin was not there. Having been an electrical engineer, David was concerned that there might be a fundamental reason for Sammie's headaches. When he inspected the premises, he was convinced that there was a major problem with the heating system which in his opinion was not sufficiently ventilated. In brief, he suspected that Sammie might be suffering from carbon monoxide poisoning. The next Monday, Sammie and I challenged Colin about this. His response was extremely negative and of course he denied any liability. I insisted that he have the equipment tested but he refused. So rather than getting into protracted legal proceedings without any definitive proof, we decided that the only thing Sammie could do was to hand in her notice with immediate effect. It came as no surprise to us that after a week or so at home, she suffered no further bouts of sickness or headaches. It seemed to me that once again fate had dealt my daughter a lousy card.

Meanwhile Sammie's anxiety attacks and bouts of depression continued. I believe it was the insecurity that these provoked in her that led her to persuade Barbara that they should enter into a civil partnership. This was a relatively new development in society's attitude to the gay community, and we were nervous about the legal aspects of such a move. But Sammie was adamant and Barbara went along with it. At this point I really had to ask myself what my own attitude was to the whole lesbian thing. She of course wanted to have a full-on ceremony, with a reception for friends and family and a night in a hotel for the two lovebirds afterwards. She naturally asked me to give her away and to make a suitable speech at the reception in the local gastro pub restaurant afterwards. I had often been called upon to take on a public speaking role but this one was a toughy! The girls dressed in matching trouser suit outfits, family and friends donned their glad rags and I gave a speech and proposed the toast to the happy couple. It all passed off without any issues, but I do recall with some horror my dear ex-wife turning to her daughter during the meal and remarking, "Do you know, this is the exact date when your father left us." To her eternal credit, Sammie rounded on her mum and replied that this was not the sort of thing to be told on her special day and could her mother please just shut up.

Sammie and Barbara resumed their life together but there was no doubt that poor Sammie was still unwell. Nevertheless, recognising the urgent need for some income, she set about rectifying this issue which was becoming a serious bone of contention between the two of them.

Sammie looked at the mournful face of her beloved Hugo and saw a possible way out. With the increasing trend of households with both partners working, she realised that there was an increasing need for someone to look after people's pets during the day, feeding cats and walking dogs until the owners returned. A friend had started a little business doing this and had a small portfolio of clients which Sammie negotiated to take over. It was in our view unlikely to produce a living wage but it would be better than nothing. So suddenly for the princely sum of £500 there she was as the proud owner of her own business, called *Pets Alone*. We lent her money again to acquire a suitable vehicle in which she could transport her canine clients, and so she set about building this business virtually from scratch.

If you've never contemplated such an undertaking, let me tell you that it can be a daunting prospect. But for someone who had been diagnosed with clinical depression and was being medically treated for this to start her own business was nothing short of remarkable. This really was the very first step in her long, painful road to recovery.

Chapter 5

Life with Barbara, cats and dogs, ups and downs, their relationship on the rocks.

BARBARA WAS AN INTERESTING CHARACTER. The daughter of north London Jewish parents, she did not have a particular religious affiliation. Her father sadly died shortly after we met Barbara. Her mother was a rather unpleasant woman who clearly did not approve of her daughter's liaison with Sammie, so her attitude to us was at best indifferent. We rather liked Barbara. She had a good sense of humour, was intelligent and shared with us a love of sport, theatre and ballet. We would often invite them both over for drinks or meals and we seemed to get on well with her, appreciating how she had to live with the vicissitudes of Sammie's mental health. But we were surprised and disappointed when, early on in their relationship, Barbara had resigned from her well-paid sales position with a large I.T. company in Hemel Hempstead, and as a result, had reduced their disposable income significantly. This, and their desire to move to a bigger house but in a cheaper area, motivated a move from Tring in Hertfordshire to Leighton Buzzard in the adjacent county of Bedfordshire. We were sorry to see them leave Tring. Sammie had made the house cosy, and with its location on a small estate right by the Grand Union Canal, it was a safe and pleasant environment.

Perhaps like Sammie, Barbara had been discriminated against. Lesbians were not often top of the popularity polls in large companies in those days. One of her passions was rugby, and it was mine too, having had a trial for England Schools in 1960. She had even been selected to play for the England women's team when she was younger, and on one occasion I went with Sammie to watch her play in a match against a local team. She played on the wing and acquitted herself efficiently. It has to be said, however, that the two of them didn't seem to share many interests in common. Sammie liked country music whilst Barbara preferred jazz. Barbara liked watching sport on TV, but Sammie preferred films. We searched in vain for activities that might help them develop mutual interests. On one occasion we took them both to the London Coliseum to see the English National Ballet perform. I think they enjoyed the experience, but it probably wasn't really Sammie's thing. So we did wonder if the relationship would be capable of lasting a lifetime.

Meanwhile, Barbara decided that she would like to find a steady job without the ups and downs of a commercial organisation. So she applied for a civilian role with the local police force in Aylesbury. After the regulation interviews and background checks, she was accepted for a position in the video monitoring section. She enjoyed this greatly, so much so that she subsequently applied for and was again accepted for a uniform role with the British Transport Police force. She joined the Euston station team in London, which was an easy commute from Leighton Buzzard, although it did involve shift work, often with unsociable hours.

I have always enjoyed playing music at home, and at the time I was enjoying the dramatic ballads of *Peter Cetera*, the former lead singer with the American band *Chicago*. For some reason the *Peter Cetera* CD always seemed to be playing when the two of them came to visit. It was only much later when we knew her well that Barbara confessed that she hated the singer and always dreaded the likelihood of him booming out through our big sound system over tea!

Throughout this period Sammie's health spiralled in and out of control again, and it became clear that things were getting out of hand. We kept in regular contact, feeling that we at least could give them both a sense of stability in what was gradually becoming an unsustainable situation. Yet there were positive aspects to it. After a great deal of hard work Sammie's little dog walking business was beginning to provide a regular income.

Sammie was also an excellent home maker. She kept the house immaculate, taking pride in their fixtures and fittings, and becoming a competent and inventive cook. We enjoyed many tasty lunches and suppers at their home, and helped them to keep their small garden as pleasant as we could. They both loved animals. In addition to Sammie's wonderful Labrador Hugo, they acquired two cats, although it has to be said that in their animal world it was rather a stand-off position, with the cats spending most of their time upstairs while Hugo occupied the ground floor! But there was no doubt that Hugo became a highly significant character in Sammie's story, and all our family came to love him as our own. At one stage they also gave a home to two rabbits. They built a cage and a little run at the bottom of their garden, and even on occasions brought the rabbits into the house for a bit of R and R!

We often wondered how they managed to pay their bills in the new house. Barbara in particular was a dreadful manager of money. She seemed to have no grasp of the necessity to live within one's means, so as in many relationships, this became an increasing bone of contention between them. Having just survived the financial crisis of the credit card bills, Sammie at least appeared to have learned her lesson and was even beginning to put a little aside. But there is no doubt that they lived from hand-to-mouth on a month by month basis. They both found pleasure in the more relaxed atmosphere in Cornwall, where they had several short holidays. I think they would both have liked to move there, but it was simply not possible given their work commitments at home.

Throughout this period their lives were on an emotional roller coaster, dictated by Sammie's precarious mental state. At times she would seem to be coping, but then the black dog would strike again and there would be another crisis. All this began to have an effect on our lives too. I remember especially the occasion when they were visiting us and Sammie was in crisis mode. She was alternately morose, aggressive and tearful, culminating in her announcement that she couldn't stand it anymore and had to leave the house immediately. I don't recall the reason for this, but I do know that I had to physically restrain her from walking out and driving off into the night. I quite literally feared for her life, and I had to force her to sit on the sofa in floods of tears yet again. It was horrible, and Jane and I were deeply affected by it. It seemed that no matter how hard we tried to help our daughter, there was nothing that either we or anyone else could do. Her elder sister found this situation extremely hard to deal with, being still in the 'for God's sake, get a grip' mode. We recall that some days after Barbara had driven Sammie home, we had a conversation with her in which we told her that if she ever felt that she couldn't take any more, we would understand if she left Sammie. But we begged her not to, fearing that it might provoke another suicide attempt. And so it proved to be.

One day Sammie rang us in complete hysterics, saying that Barbara had started a relationship with another woman and wanted out of their civil partnership. It made me recall the circumstances of the termination of my first marriage, and how very difficult it had been for everyone involved to cope with that trauma. They started to live separate lives but still living in the same house. It must have been the final straw for Sammie, who had endured years of anxiety and depression and could now see her life falling apart. We did our best to look after her. We attended several meetings with the Crisis Care team at the local mental health clinic, who had been called to their house on several occasions. Their support, whilst intermittent, did seem to be helping Sammie come to terms with her situation, although by this time she was heavily dependent on her drugs regime.

One weekend our neighbour, who runs the local Riding for the Disabled, organised a Fun Dog Show as a fund-raising event. We brought our grandchildren over, and they all loved seeing the different breeds of dogs taking part. But during the event, we received a telephone call to say that Sammie had been taken to hospital once again after yet another attempt on her life. I rushed over and found her emotionally exhausted and, quite frankly, ready to give up all hope of ever recovering. But recover she did, sufficiently at least to return home. And so the roller coaster continued relentlessly. Jane and I clung to each other for support, feeling hopeless and helpless, not knowing what we could do.

By now it was clear that the girls had come to the end of the road and could no longer live together. We advised Sammie to stay put but she said it was just too painful listening to Barbara talking on the phone to her new lady, and spending more and more time away from home. So she found a small terraced cottage at the other end of town to rent unfurnished. We had to guarantee the rental which we did, and so we helped her move out and in. That was yet another painful moment for the three of us. Sammie arrived with a few bits of crockery, some bedding and not much else. We bought her a cheap sofa to sit on in the evenings. God, it was awful. The cottage was right on a main road, had two small bedrooms upstairs and a lounge and kitchen on the ground floor. There was a narrow garden at the back, and I recall attending to a rose bush, the only flower in the place, so that it might provide some colour in the summertime.

In all the years we had lived with Sammie's illness, this was the worst time. I felt so sorry for her, because it seemed that while the other members of our family had created loving families for themselves, poor Sammie seemed incapable of gaining any lasting happiness in her life. And now, we wondered what the future could possibly hold for her. She was alone in a pretty horrible place, both physically and emotionally. Well, not quite alone, she had Jane and me and the family. Oh, and Hugo.

It was not long before Sammie came to the conclusion that if she could not get some stability into her life, there really was no future for her. Jane and I spoke to Barbara who had visited the cottage and seen the state that Sammie was in, and asked her if she would do a swap so that Sammie and Hugo could return to the home they both loved. Eventually, to our great relief, Barbara agreed, and so Sammie and Hugo found themselves back in their home. Once more, we all heaved a massive sigh of relief.

Chapter 6

Sammie finds her feet...with the help of Hugo and Pets Alone. A new relationship begins, and we see the first signs of recovery.

JANE AND I WERE NERVOUS about Sammie having to live on her own, look after the house and run her business. The only thing we were confident about was that Hugo would be cared for. Up to this point, I have to say that most times in her life she would prevaricate rather than make a decision, and even if she did make a decision the next challenge would be for her to act on it. But faced with the reality of life alone, she quickly realised that the solution lay with *Pets Alone.* Through a combination of hard work, determination and word of mouth, her business slowly started to become a going concern. Clients liked her and would also seek her advice on all aspects of pet ownership. In addition to walking the dogs, she would also visit people's houses to feed their cats, so the days were pretty full-on. But as with all small businesses, it seemed that no sooner had she managed to put a few pounds away for a rainy day, then it would start to pour! There were often minor issues with the house, but it was the *Pets Alone* van that proved to be a rapidly declining asset. Servicing and repairs would quickly take care of any monthly surplus income, but since without that the business would collapse, it was essential to keep the van on the road.

Because Sammie lived on a large estate, she had to find a more suitable space where her clients' dogs could be exercised. But when it came to the business she was becoming increasingly resourceful, so it wasn't long before she discovered a delightful area west of Leighton Buzzard with the rather exotic name of Heath and Reach. She would frequently arrive in the trusty van with anything up to six dogs in tow! We occasionally used to pop over there and accompany her on her walks, and I was impressed with the confident manner in which she coped with her precious cargo.

One of the things we learned about depression is that inactivity is its real enemy. But sufferers of depression are by their very nature prone to inactivity. They find it hard to summon up the motivation to get out of bed in the morning, so it becomes something of a vicious circle. We could see that *Pets Alone* was giving Sammie a reason to carry on, and we certainly began to notice a decline in the depressive moments to which we had become accustomed for so many years. Could we dare to wonder, we thought, if she was actually beginning to turn a corner?

I mentioned Hugo, but he's certainly worth more than just a mention! That wonderfully loyal and supportive animal proved to be a lifeline for Sammie. Now that she was living on her own, Hugo was her only daily companion, with her from morning until night sharing her sorrow and literally caring for her during bouts of depression. He would accompany her on her dog-walking twice a day, and stay quietly in the van when she was attending to people's pets in their own homes. He would sit with her on the sofa as a companion in the evenings and snuggle up to her on (and sometimes even in!) the bed through the night. And when she was away from the house and he was left on his own, he would just have a snooze and wait patiently for her return. I can honestly say that I doubt whether Sammie could have coped without Hugo in the early stages of her life on her own. Nowadays dogs are increasingly being used in a therapeutic way, comforting the sick and providing companionship for the elderly and infirm, and this was certainly the role that he performed so completely for our Sammie. Dear Hugo!

By now Sammie was under the care of the local authority's mental health unit, which seemed to us to do the best they could with the limited resources they had at their disposal. Sammie was assigned a qualified carer who established something of a rapport with her. Although the sessions were always time-restricted, she was at least getting the support she clearly still needed. Her medication was also being regulated in order to establish the optimum dose. As I mentioned earlier, she had been diagnosed with something called Borderline Personality Disorder. We had no idea what this was, other than at the time it seemed that mental health issues were being continually re-categorised into numerous newly defined conditions. This one sounded from its title as if she was only just on the cusp of a particular condition, but on researching it we discovered that it was something quite different. To quote a reputable online source, '*Borderline Personality Disorder is a mental illness marked by an ongoing pattern of varying moods, self-image, and behaviour.*

These symptoms often result in impulsive actions and problems in relationships. People with Borderline Personality Disorder may experience intense episodes of anger, depression and anxiety that can last from a few hours to days.' Got it in one!

Sammie started attending classes in 'mindfulness', an increasingly popular technique which, in the words of another online source, is 'An awareness of our thoughts and feelings as they happen moment to moment. It's about allowing ourselves to see the present moment clearly. When we do that, it can positively change the way we see ourselves and our lives.' Okay. Not quite sure how it works, but we began to see slow but gradual improvements in the way that Sammie was dealing with day-to-day problems, organising her life and generally showing signs of improving well-being. Halleluyah!

We were also impressed by her learning-on-the-job skills and increasing experience of dealing with domestic animals, especially dogs and cats. She had previously taken a course in canine water therapies and so was extremely confident in handling any physical problem or situation she encountered. It was clear to us that her clients were really impressed with her, and some even became personal friends.

One of her clients was an American lady who was married to an Englishman in the Royal Air Force. They had recently arrived from the States where he had been previously posted, and they now lived a few doors down from Sammie. One Christmas, this lady's sister arrived to visit England for the first time. Sammie met her and it quickly became apparent that there was a mutual attraction. We were somewhat wary of this new liaison, coming as it did not so long after the failure of her previous relationship. One of the characteristics of BPD sufferers is an all-or-nothing approach to life, and this was certainly in evidence in the rapidity with which these two people formed an attachment. The result was a transatlantic romance via video which blossomed over the following months, culminating in Sammie accepting an invitation to visit Carolyn in her home in Cleveland, Ohio. Sammie's sister Eve was equally concerned and advised her to take things more slowly, but all to no avail. Sammie had made up her mind that she would go, and nothing we said or did was going to stop her.

It came as something of a surprise when we spoke to Sammie shortly after she arrived. It seemed that Carolyn had virtually ignored her from the moment of her arrival. She had made absolutely no plans to entertain her, to show her around the area or to introduce her to her friends. To us this was bizarre behaviour, but it was the first of numerous examples of the cavernous gap between Carolyn's lifestyle and our own. I think Sammie was actually rather lonely on that trip. Carolyn worked in the caring profession providing counselling for troubled children. When we began to learn more about her own behaviour and lifestyle, we could hardly believe that she was studying for a Master's Degree in the subject, when she was so clearly incapable of controlling her own behaviour. More of this later.

Sammie returned to the UK, chastened but still convinced that there was a serious relationship blossoming between her and Carolyn. We disagreed, but simply tried to support her emotionally in what she obviously thought was a whole new exciting phase of her life. In retrospect, perhaps we should have reacted more decisively, and given that Jane and I had also previously been officially appointed as her carers, simply told her that this was not a suitable person for her to associate with. But we had reckoned without a more fundamental issue that I touched on in a previous chapter, being the difference between Sammie and her siblings.

She was my younger daughter and her education had been interrupted by the bullying at school which led to her poor exam results. She was not living with us at that stage, and frankly she did not receive much support from her mother, who herself had been poorly educated in her childhood. On the other hand, Eve was a bright, personable child, determined to succeed in everything she did. She went on to have a successful business career, got married and had two beautiful daughters. My step-son Daniel was a lovely lad with a God-given gift of making everyone like him. He was good-looking, married a pretty girl, had two daughters of his own and built a highly successful business to boot. So, I can imagine that Sammie must have sometimes felt that life had dealt her a rotten set of cards, given what her siblings were achieving. She was perhaps desperate to prove to us, to them and to herself that she too could make something of her life despite the setbacks of her childhood. Inevitably she saw Carolyn as the route to a whole new future, perhaps even in a new country, where she could turn over a new leaf and create a new life for herself. We cannot blame her for thinking that, although she has always maintained that there was genuine love between her and Carolyn, despite what we all saw as the blindingly obvious danger signs which were later to prove disastrous.

Chapter 7

Dealing with death. Will Sammie be able to cope?

I'M FINDING THIS CHAPTER VERY difficult to write. Which is puzzling, because the trauma of Sammie's illness has been difficult enough to relive, and that is of course the main thrust of this story.

We were aware that Tina had been unwell for some time both because the girls would talk about their visits to her and David, and also because we would see them both on their visits to Eve and her husband Justin at Christmas time. She always seemed so small and frail, and perhaps a little uneasy in my presence. When her condition deteriorated, we realized that it was just a matter of time before she passed away. But death is the ultimate finality, and when it comes it brings with it a tsunami of emotions for those who are left behind. I remember with surprise my own reaction to the news of my first wife's death. I was visiting our daughter-in-law Christine when the phone call came through. It was Sammie who telephoned, and of course she was in floods of tears. It was only later that Jane and I were to learn of the deeply upsetting circumstances of her death, but to hear my younger daughter sobbing on the phone provoked an instant reaction of emotion for which I was unprepared. I finished the call by reminding Sammie that we were always there for her, then turned to Christine and said, "Tina just died."

The full meaning of the phrase suddenly hit me and my eyes welled up. I sat down, and Christine gave me a loving embrace. Tina was, after all, the mother of my two daughters and the woman I had spent eight years with, albeit with the constant realisation that I had made a mistake in marrying her. Her passing brought back the feelings of sadness that I have always felt. And most of all, despair at having to leave my children with a woman who was so obviously incapable of coping with motherhood. Worse than that as we subsequently realised, someone who was incapable of ever showing love and support for her two daughters. She just couldn't do it. And as I like to think of myself as a fundamentally warm and caring person I found that so difficult to understand.

Some years after our divorce, the girls told me that their mother had actually said that having her daughters had ruined her life. How could anyone be that callous? I think what she meant was that she had to give up her quasi-glamorous job in a London public relations agency and exchange it for the responsibility of everything that being a mother entails. But I found that very hard to come to terms with. It's a generally accepted fact that women have an innate biological desire to procreate. Without this, the human race would be heading for extinction. But it's also a fact that there are a few women who simply have no desire to produce children. Perhaps they have had a bad experience in childhood or are too focused on their careers, who knows? And unfortunately, I have come to realise that my first wife fell into this category.

Writing this has in a strange way helped me to overcome some of the emotions I have described, but the fact is that Tina changed from the minute Eve arrived from the vivacious, fun-loving London girl about town whom I married, to someone who was completely adrift in a sea of personal recrimination and self-pity. It was just too much for me, and I could not entertain the idea of spending the rest of my life with someone like that. But yes, at the moment of her death I felt pity for her. She had quickly decided that she was incapable of looking after herself on her own, let alone her two girls, and had embarked on a personal journey to find a replacement for me as soon as she possibly could. Thank goodness she found a kind and gentle man who, God knows how, seemed able to cope with her moods and her excesses.

It was also deeply distressing for Jane and me to see how the girls were affected by their mother's death. And of course, the timing, on Christmas Eve of all days, could hardly have been worse. The days and nights they had spent by her bedside in hospital must have been completely traumatising for them, and we were both filled with a desire to comfort and support them when they returned home, both emotionally battered by the experience. By all accounts this death was the stuff of nightmares, from which I know they both suffered for many months afterwards, and unfortunately would remember every Christmas.

We made the best we could of that Christmas Day, all of us including

Justin's parents who had become our good friends, trying to be festive without it seeming disrespectful to those who were in shock and in mourning. Then came the funeral. Having passed away at the very beginning of the Christmas holiday period, it seemed that all the services associated with such a trauma simply shut down. It was over a week before the funeral director returned to work, and as a consequence there was the inevitable backlog before a day could be found for a cremation service.

The girls asked us both to attend, and we naturally agreed so that we could support them as best we could. Tina had insisted on a non-religious service, and Eve managed to find a gentleman who specialised in conducting such events. He merely asked Eve to furnish him with some facts about her mother, which provided him with a basic framework to work from. The girls were too upset to consider giving a eulogy and David was not up to the task, so it was left to the service convener. In retrospect he did an admirable job, allowing for some embellishment of the facts he had been given, and a certain amount of repeated information. I held Sammie's hand throughout the service, knowing that Eve had her husband to comfort her.

Looking back, I think that Tina simply gave up on life once she had children. But why? When I met her, she appeared intelligent and capable of achieving much in her life. But after becoming a mother she made no attempt to rebuild her life. With her talents and experience she could easily have been a senior, valued executive in a regional business, and that would have given her the stimulation she was obviously lacking. And that made me feel extremely sad too. Since that time, Jane and I have done everything we can to alleviate the pain that the girls must have felt, both at the death of their mum at a relatively young age by today's standards, and at the manner of her passing.

It is now some years afterwards, and their pain has perhaps been replaced by acceptance. Certainly, I feel both girls have come to terms with the lack of love they received as children, and I hope that Jane and I have compensated for it. I know Sammie sees Jane as her substitute mum, and I'm sure that Eve feels the same way. And inevitably, Tina's death also reminded me of my own parents. My mother had worked incredibly hard all her life to help my father build a successful hotel business, but this was cruelly cut short by a massive heart attack at the age of 60 which very nearly killed her. She was told that she should stop work immediately, and so had to retire from the Devonshire hotel they had worked so hard to make a success. They decided to buy a small house in Maidenhead where my mother could stay whilst they tried to sell the hotel, which was near my school in Oxford, where they could both eventually retire to once the business had been sold. But her health never fully recovered, and my father found it difficult to run the business without the support and presence of his wife. When the hotel was eventually disposed of prematurely they decided to settle in Norfolk, the county of my mother's birth. I'm sure she knew she didn't have long to live, and a few years later, she died in my father's arms of another massive heart attack. She was 65, I was 25. She had at least hung on through sheer determination to see me married, but my father never got over the shock of losing her in that way. He lived for a few more years, moved to Buckinghamshire to be near us and having been a lifelong smoker died in a nursing home from throat cancer. So, by my mid-thirties I had lost both my parents, and the news of Tina's early death brought it all back and produced the reaction I have described.

Chapter 8

Life after a death. Learning about Carolyn.
Sammie's actually going to move!

WE WERE CONSTANTLY AWARE THAT Sammie's mental state was fragile, and dreaded the thought of a possible relapse into depression again. So when my first wife died, there was the very real possibility of this happening. But we were relieved when she seemed to regard this sad event as the end of a chapter in her life, and therefore the start of a new one. She had been very affected by what she perceived as her mum's unhealthy lifestyle, so she set about improving her own, both mentally and physically. She started going to the gym, which both surprised and delighted us. Visits did seem to be a bit sporadic at first, but once she started to see some weight loss, she began to feel better. As we all know, this cycle becomes a virtuous circle, just as easily as the converse when people make no effort and it becomes harder and harder to arrest their mental and physical decline. So, in a way, her mum had finally had a positive influence on Sammie, and I'm sure that by taking regular exercise it helped her to come to terms with her loss.

Meanwhile it was also clear that this new relationship of hers was becoming serious. We have never been able to work out whether it was a genuine romance or if she was simply clutching at straws, so desperate was she to turn her life around. To be honest, none of our family had been impressed with Carolyn when we first met her. It's hard to find the right words, but there was just something rather odd about her. One thing I do remember was that when she visited us at our home and we would give her a glass of wine, she would lose no time in replenishing her glass without being invited to do so. She would just go to the fridge and help herself to another.

On one occasion at Christmas time, she brought her mother over to England to stay with her sister. We naturally felt that we should entertain the lady while she was here, and as this was her first-ever visit to the UK, we decided to take her, Sammie and Carolyn on a trip to one of this country's most spectacular stately homes. Waddesdon Manor is the ancestral home in England of the Rothschild family, the fabulously wealthy dynasty that had made their fortune predominantly from banking. They were intelligent, cultured and great philanthropists too, building houses for their workers and creating whole new towns in Buckinghamshire and Hertfordshire. The family home, which is still occupied by the descendants, had been signed over to the National Trust, a highly regarded charity which cares for hundreds of historic houses as well as thousands of acres of British countryside, thus contributing to the historic culture of this nation. Waddesdon is a most spectacular estate and is generally regarded as the jewel in the crown of the National Trust. So, I thought, what better place to take our American guests for a day out in England?

It was, however, pretty clear from the outset that we had misread our visitors' likes and dislikes. Whenever we have taken friends to Waddesdon Manor, they have all immediately been delighted by the sight of the house and gardens, which are designed in the style of a French chateau, reflecting the Rothschild's family and business connections with that country. To be brutally honest, all this went completely over the heads of our guests, who made absolutely no comment at all on any of the beautiful, historical and priceless artifacts they saw. It was clear that Carolyn's background was very different to our own, but for Sammie's sake we persevered and entertained them as best we could.

I've spent some time on this because not for the first time we had serious misgivings about the way this relationship was going. We felt that Sammie was being rather naïve and was frankly blinded by the prospect of a transatlantic romance. It was looking like another example of the all-or-nothing approach to life that we had all seen before.

Soon it was time for Sammie to make another visit to Cleveland. One redeeming feature of Carolyn's personality was that she had a relatively well-paid job as a counsellor for troubled young adults, and we were impressed to hear that she was studying for a Master's Degree in Couples Counselling. But when Sammie returned from her latest trip, we were alarmed to hear about the lady's lifestyle. It was clear that she was a heavy drinker, but more worrying was that she apparently would ignore the drink and drive laws, using the old cliché that she was perfectly capable of controlling her vehicle even after several beers and glasses of wine. I know that Sammie found this particularly difficult to handle but worse was to come. Apparently, there was a lodger in the house who was a regular user of soft drugs, something that I'm certain Sammie has never done, and she used to comment on how the characteristic aroma of a regular pot smoker would waft through the house whenever he was around. Just what was our daughter getting into, we wondered? Needless to say, both we and Sammie's elder sister Eve tried to point out the reality of this situation, but the lady was not for turning. She had by now decided that there was no future for her in England, and that she wanted to live with Carolyn in America. Jane and I tried our best to be neutral in our opinion of this because we could see that Sammie was entering a new phase of her life, but it seemed to us that she was hurtling towards yet another disaster emotionally and financially.

Some time later, Sammie announced that she and Carolyn were getting engaged, and that she was commencing proceedings to apply for a visa to live and work in the States. She planned to save up for a ring for Carolyn, and had completed the necessary papers for the application. She had even found a potential buyer for *Pets Alone*, so this was now a reality. I guess in a way this situation reminded me of the very difficult time when Jane and I first got together and my first wife rapidly remarried. This meant that instead of my being about 12 miles away from my girls, I was 180 miles away after their move up north. Now, we were going to be not tens, not hundreds, but thousands of miles from Sammie, and given the family's general attitude to her move, we couldn't be sure when we would be seeing her again. Even up to this point I think we doubted whether she would really go. There was the question of *Pets Alone* which still needed to be sold, and there was the major issue of Hugo. He was still playing an important part in her recovery from depression but could he accompany her on this long journey? What would it cost her to take the dog with her, and how would Hugo cope with such a stressful event?

Well, we had reckoned without our daughter's determination. Once she received her visa, she set about solving all the logistical problems involved. She found someone who wanted to take on the business and negotiated a price. She sold her van and some of her possessions. She researched which airlines were prepared to fly an animal across the Atlantic and how exactly it would happen. These were major, life-changing decisions, and up to this point Jane and I had felt that Sammie was just not up to the task of coping with them. We were wrong. In fact, the family actually started making bets on how long this relationship would last, because we were all convinced that it was not right for her. But we had to admit that we had reckoned without her new-found determination. Sammie started, perhaps for the first time in her life, to display some of the tenacity and maturity needed to make it all work, and despite our advice not to undertake this journey, it became clear that her mind was made up. She was going to go with Hugo to a new life in a country with, frankly, more differences than similarities to England, with only Carolyn to meet her. We did not like the prospect of her going, but she was absolutely determined to try and start a new life, and there was nothing we could do or say to dissuade her.

Chapter 9

Sammie says goodbye… we say 'why?'

SAMMIE HAD HER VISA, SO was ready to go to America. Once again we were faced with the reality of my younger daughter, with her long history of mental illness, acting irrationally as it seemed to the rest of the family, and going to live in a foreign country with a partner whose character and behaviour had not impressed us, where we would no longer be able to provide the support and care that we had done for many years previously. It was deeply troubling, but we knew enough about Sammie now to realise that once she had set her mind to do something, there was little that we or anyone else could do to dissuade her. We all felt it was the wrong move for her but we recognised the reasons for her decision. So there was nothing for it but to go along with her plan and support her as best we could up to the moment of departure. I knew also that the two sisters had become much closer since their mother's death, and I worried that their parting would be very emotional and upsetting for both of them.

Sammie had established that the only airline prepared to transport dogs in the hold of a transatlantic flight was *Virgin Airways*, so her passage was duly booked. Both *Pets Alone* and the house jointly owned with Barbara were sold and the contents dealt with. Naturally Jane and I told Sammie we would drive her to Heathrow Airport, where she had firstly to check Hugo in with the animal cargo section. I hired a van with a crate, and early in the morning went to pick it up, then drove to Eve and Justin's house in Berkhamsted where Sammie had spent her last night in the UK. To be honest, none of us knew how long she would last in Ohio, nor when any of us would be seeing her again. Jane and I had prepared ourselves for this moment, rationalising that this was a game-changing adventure for Sammie, and if it didn't work out, she could always come back. But to what? With little money, no home and no job, her prospects seemed pretty hopeless, and inevitably we were concerned that if that were the case it could affect her emotional stability.

Her sister Eve was deeply upset on two counts. Firstly, she was convinced that Sammie was going for the wrong reasons and that the relationship which had been fostered largely on the internet was bound to fail. Secondly, as I have said, they were both still grieving for their mother, whose death had hit them both very hard. Eve suddenly realised that the loss of their mum had forged a bond that had brought the two sisters closer to each other than they had ever been given their different characters and lifestyles. Eve was visibly distressed, and had long conversations with her little sister about their lives and how they now needed to support each other emotionally. She promised Sammie that if she had to come back, there would be a bed for her in Berkhamsted while she tried to rebuild her life.

Soon it was time to leave for the airport. We all tried to keep it low-key whilst we loaded Hugo into his crate in the van, but we were all holding back the tears. Watching Eve, Sammie and the girls hugging and sobbing was deeply affecting for us, but we had to hold ourselves together to be strong for both of them. The journey to Heathrow is always stressful as it entails travelling on one of the busiest stretches of Britain's over-crowded motorways. It can take anything from 40 minutes to nearly 2 hours. But luck was with us on that day and we arrived in good time. Firstly, we had to locate the animal centre which was some distance away from the main terminals, wait for it to open, and then complete the formalities for Hugo's transportation. We were informed that once he was in the airline crate, he would not be allowed out until they were delivered to the equivalent animal reception centre in New York, which would be anything from 8 to 12 hours. This really affected Sammie, and so it was again heart-rending to watch her say goodbye to her faithful companion. We drove to the departure terminal in pieces. We agreed that we would follow our normal routine of saying goodbye on the tarmac outside the terminal, and so, with heavy hearts, we wished our Sammie well as she set out on another chapter of her eventful life.

We drove back along the M25 motorway feeling pretty miserable, but to make matters worse, just as we came off the motorway and up to the traffic lights on the main road, the rented van coughed, spluttered and came to a halt at the front of the traffic line! Other motorists on their way to work in the middle of the morning rush hour had to push the van while I tried to start it on the clutch, but it was having none of it. Horns inevitably started hooting and we were left pushed up onto the kerb while I telephoned the van rental company. They sent a pick-up truck which took 40 minutes to arrive whilst we stood at the side of the road and fielded a long series of furious looks from delayed commuters. Just what we needed after the morning's harrowing events! We eventually reached the van depot, transferred to our car, drove home and poured ourselves a large drink! Now it was just a matter of waiting until she arrived at her new home, and we occupied ourselves as best we could until we could speak to her and hear how the journey had gone for her and poor Hugo.

Chapter 10

Sammie settles in, but we sense all is not well.

DESPITE OUR VIEW THAT SAMMIE had jumped headlong into the frying pan and might well find herself in the fire, as her parents we had to continue to support her emotionally, albeit from afar. Thank goodness for video calling. This was the first time that we had used the service extensively, and of course we loved it. We developed a little ritual for our conversations with Sammie, which happened every few days. We both quickly worked out what times of the day were most suitable to speak to each other, although it seemed quite rare that Carolyn would be present and would join in the conversation. The ritual, developed quite naturally, was that at the end of every conversation we would finish by each saying 'love you loads', to which the other party would reply, 'love you too'. It was a small thing but it meant that whatever the topic of conversation, the sessions would always end on a positive note. Perhaps something to remember if you're a parent of a depressive child.

At first, we could sense Sammie's excitement at having finally achieved the objective of living in America with the lady with whom she had told us all she wanted to spend the rest of her life. But gradually we began to realise that the reality was very different from the dream. She described how Carolyn still had her lodger Jimmy, which for newly married people seemed to us a bit odd. But we put it down to financial reasons which was perhaps reasonable at the time. But then Sammie began to describe the lifestyles of both Carolyn and Jimmy, the latter's being centred around drink, drugs and cigarettes. This was definitely not the environment that she had expected, and naturally it raised questions in our mind once more about Sammie's poor judgement in this whole endeavour.

Sammie's first hurdle was getting an American driving license and then a temporary work permit, but happily she was able to achieve this after about six months. We also reminded ourselves that after the long years of depression and anxiety she had suffered, it had left her with a fear of working in an office situation. I put this down to the prejudice she had encountered once her school and work colleagues realised that she was gay. Things have changed radically now in that regard, but in those days just a few years ago, there was a definite gulf between gay and straight people.

The first piece of good news was that she found a job that really suited her. It meant working outside with dogs trained to scare Canada geese away from parks and other public and private spaces in Cleveland, and it was a heaven-sent opportunity for her. It did not involve sitting in an office with other people, which suited her mental state perfectly. The experience she had gained with *Pets Alone* became immediately apparent to the owners of the geese control company and she quickly established herself as one of their best dog handlers. So that was one problem solved.

Meanwhile it was becoming increasingly apparent that her home life was not what she had expected. A partner with a chaotic lifestyle and a lodger who clearly had considerable problems of his own was not the ideal setting for a happy married life. But there was also another issue which emerged from our online conversations. Carolyn had clearly no concept of personal financial management, and was prone to bouts of irrational expenditure which was putting pressure both on their household budget and as a result, on their relationship. I thought, *God, here we go again*. But after the excesses of her previous life, Sammie was determined to act more responsibly when it came to finances and she was now extremely careful about any unnecessary expenditure. So it was with horror that we learned that her wife had transferred all the money she had deposited in their joint account, some $10,000, into her personal account. She had apparently done this because she was concerned about the fragility of their relationship and wanted to protect herself! I thought this was quite frankly despicable, and tantamount to theft. It appeared that she had basically stolen the money, and had done so without telling Sammie. This was a turning point for us.

Carolyn then announced that they were going to move from their rented home and that she was going to buy a property. We urged Sammie not to become a joint owner, but she needed no reminding of the now precarious position she was once again in, both financially and emotionally, and had already told Carolyn that she did not want to be a co-owner.

It was obvious from all of this that their relationship was in trouble, so Jane and I decided to go and see for ourselves.

Chapter 11

An unexpected surprise! But things go from bad to worse. We decide it's time to find out for ourselves.

WE WERE SOMEWHAT AMAZED TO hear that Sammie had done a rather unusual thing. She had read somewhere that the President receives thousands of letters, texts and emails every day, so on a whim she decided to write to him to thank him for changing the laws relating to same sex relationships. She told him how much she loved living in America and that she was hoping to spend the rest of her life there. She received a reply from the White House staff saying that every communication is read by a specialist team, and that just three messages are selected each day to receive a personal reply from the President. So imagine her amazement and delight when she was told that hers had been selected! Sure enough, a few days later she received an email from President Obama, thanking her for her sentiments and replying in a way that was clearly not a standard response but one which had been personally dictated. If you've got this far, you will have read the text of the President's letter. What a wonderful boost this gave her! It seemed therefore that after the latest tragedy in her personal life, things were once more looking a little more positive. The roller coaster was rolling again, but this time in the right direction.

Nevertheless, it had become clear to us that this woman whom Sammie had married seemed irrational and unstable. We were constantly amazed and appalled at some of the things that were going on, which we had related to us on our frequent video conversations. Much of the problem in the relationship appeared to stem from Carolyn's apparent dependence on alcohol. I don't know if she would be officially diagnosed as an alcoholic, but this was clearly a constant bone of contention between them. Even through her darkest days of depression and anxiety, Sammie had never taken much to drink and for this we were very grateful and relieved. Furthermore, we were all too aware of the spiral of dependency that comes from a drugs habit, but to our knowledge none of our children, especially Sammie, had ever succumbed to that particular habit. Again, huge sighs of relief all round. But from the descriptions of Carolyn's drinking habits and consequent behaviour, a pattern of verbal abuse was emerging that we felt could spell the end of their relationship. But then, yet another mini crisis emerged. After a conversation with her sister, Carolyn had become emotional and had announced that she wanted to have a child. We could not think of anyone less suited to the responsibilities of motherhood, and we told Sammie that she should resist this crazy idea at once. By all accounts Carolyn lived her life like a stupid, irresponsible teenager. She could not keep to any timetable and constantly showed up late for most social occasions. She was reckless in her use of alcohol, including driving when she was over the limit. And she was subject to mood swings, all characteristics of someone who had not fully matured. And this was a woman in her thirties!

Sammie quickly hit the idea of motherhood on the head, but another potential crisis had appeared, in the shape of a lump in her breast. Jane was able to talk to her from personal experience as she had also suffered the same condition, and reassure her that it was probably a cyst. She explained to Sammie that many women have to face this condition but that it did not necessarily mean she would be diagnosed with cancer. Having said that, it was a nervous time for all of us, and once again we felt the physical separation made it all the more difficult for us all to deal with it. Thankfully, after a mammogram she was declared free of cancer risk as it was simply a cyst which was rapidly dealt with. Another crisis averted!

What did surprise and impress us through all of these traumas was how Sammie was dealing with them. When she was in the UK, she was quite frankly unable to face even the smallest difficulty, but there she was dealing with an unhappy marriage and a potentially life-threatening medical situation without it causing a return to the dark days of depression. We increasingly saw examples of how she was able to cope with all these difficult situations, and we were proud of her for that.

It was clear, however, that Sammie's and Carolyn's relationship was on the rocks, so we decided it was time for us to see if there was anything that could salvage it, or indeed if it was worth salvaging. We decided to visit her in Cleveland for a few days, and thought that we would invite them both to come away with us for a couple of nights to a nice hotel somewhere in Ohio where we could all have a frank discussion. Besides which, Jane and I were missing Sammie and Hugo and had always planned to visit her in America.

Sammie was thrilled when we told her that we were coming to Cleveland. She had always hoped we would go over there so she could show us her new home and introduce us to her new friends. After an emotional reunion at the airport, we arrived at the hotel she had booked for us. It was in a very pleasant neighbourhood adjacent to a shopping mall where we had a nice informal supper in one of the many restaurants there. The next day Sammie took us to their new house. It was not in a pleasant area, but clearly offered them more space. Carolyn was at work, but greeted us later like long-lost friends. However, she was obviously busy with her work and her Master's Degree studies because we saw little of her during our stay.

We had pre-booked tickets for a classical music concert one night, and invited them both out for dinner beforehand to make it a special occasion. But when we arrived at the house Carolyn was still in bed! We thought this rather odd, but assumed she would appear shortly. We obviously didn't know her, because it was 45 minutes later when she finally made it downstairs. She had on an extremely tight dress which was totally inappropriate for someone of her build, and had plastered her face with make-up and lipstick. She was also rather tense, and clearly anxious about spending the evening with us. We had to rush the meal but even then, it was obvious that we were never going to make the venue in time. We ended up standing at the back of the hall for the whole of the first half before we could get to our front row seats. We learned later from Sammie that this behaviour was typical of the way Carolyn conducted herself, and we were not impressed.

Each day Sammie would regale us with the latest state of the relationship, and it got so bad that we were convinced that there was a disaster looming. We decided that spending two nights in a hotel with Carolyn was a step too far for us so we cancelled the planned trip to a hotel. We didn't want to leave Sammie in this situation, so decided to try and help them salvage something out of the mess they had got themselves into. We honestly tried to find the positives in their life together but it was pretty hard to do that. We invited them both out for a meal on our last night, but were frankly amazed to receive a hand-written note from Carolyn at the hotel saying that she couldn't face such a meeting given the current circumstances. This was really rather extraordinary, and we decided to insist that we got together for a face-to-face discussion. So that

Carolyn wouldn't feel outnumbered, I suggested that she ask her mum and step-dad too, and with a bit of persuasion she agreed.

The meeting was held in their house, and you could cut the atmosphere with a knife. I have chaired some difficult business meetings in my career but this was entirely new territory. Jane and I had decided to be as neutral as possible so that both girls could express their opinions and try to resolve a way forward. Mother obviously had other ideas. She started berating Sammie for the way she had treated her daughter, whereupon Carolyn also verbally attacked Sammie to such an extent that they were both shouting at each other whilst in floods of tears. It was like a scene from a bad television soap! Then there was a knock on the door and in came the step-father, a little black man who had apparently spent time in prison. I thought, *just what has our daughter got herself into here?* After seeing the situation and listening to the increasingly fractious arguments on both sides, his sole contribution was, "Well ah don' know jackshit about this kinda thing, but I think you two folks should just take yo'selves off into the kitchen and sort yo'selves out!"

At this point we called time, since it was patently obvious that the whole meeting was descending into farce, or should I perhaps say tragedy. Mindful of the practical realities of our daughter's situation, we finally asked them both to give their relationship one last attempt, which they reluctantly agreed to do. At this point the meeting ended. Back at the hotel we reviewed the situation and came to the pretty obvious conclusion that this marriage was dead in the water. Whilst I am sure that Sammie was not entirely blameless, it was abundantly clear that the two of them had nothing in common and that Carolyn had genuine personality problems which were probably a result of her background and upbringing, exacerbated by her apparent dependence on alcohol. When we first met her in England, we could see that her attitude to life was very different to ours, but we tried to believe that there was another side to her that would make the relationship work. Now we knew that this was never going to happen. After the meeting Sammie came over to the hotel, obviously emotional and upset, and we sat down to talk things through. Our advice was to seek an end to the marriage as soon as possible, and to try and build a new life for herself without Carolyn. We knew she loved living in America. She loved her new job and it was obvious that her employers liked her too, and she had made some lovely kind friends whom we met, so we felt that there could be a future for her there. But first there was the prospect of several weeks of confrontation and disputes over how to end the relationship, and we were once again faced with the possibility of Sammie's illness returning because of all the stress she would have to endure over the coming months.

In spite of all of this, we felt there was light at the end of the tunnel. We were impressed with the way Sammie had obviously taken to the American way of life and had made many warm-hearted friends. They say that like attracts like! We enjoyed meals out together, Jane was taken for a trip on the lake with Sammie's lovely boss while I played golf with her husband. I had to play with his wife's clubs which were steel-shafted and so quite different to my clubs back home. Consequently my golf was terrible, which seemed at the time to be something of a metaphor for Sammie's situation. She had got herself well and truly into the rough, and no amount of hacking would get her out of it!

But there were also some happy events during our trip. We were invited to a meal at one of her friend's home with all the family in attendance. It was a typical American family gathering, with grace said before the meal and a real feeling of mutual fellowship. And it was such a pleasure for us to see Sammie enjoying the company of her new friends. We also enjoyed an impromptu takeaway meal at her employers' house and were able to meet several other friends and employees.

Another highlight of our visit was when Sammie, Jane and I enjoyed a morning at the world-famous Cleveland Rock & Roll Hall of Fame, which houses such musical gems as *Michael Jackson's* costumes, *Ringo Starr's* first drum kit and *Pink Floyd's* pigs which they used in their spectacular live shows. I know, we've seen them live in concert twice!

But after our short visit when the time came to say goodbye, we knew that the writing was on the wall for their relationship. We gave Sammie as much comfort and support as we could, but returned to England full of foreboding at what the outcome of this situation would be for her, and once again felt somewhat helpless because of the distance between our two homes.

C h a p t e r   1 2

More momentous events for her to deal with.

A SHORT WHILE LATER WE were relieved to hear that Sammie had found a one-bedroom apartment to rent on the ground floor of a complex in a nice part of town. With a shared swimming pool and gym, it seemed the ideal spot for her to recover from the trauma of separation from Carolyn. But there was always the nagging doubt in our minds as to whether she could cope on her own. The last time that had happened was after her marriage to Barbara ended, and that was a traumatic time for everyone. Would her mental health be able to cope with a similar situation, we wondered?

The first reports we had were encouraging. Sammie described how she had coped with leaving Carolyn's house, with a mixture of emotions but mainly a feeling of sadness that the relationship had not worked out and despite our attempts to help, they had been unable to resolve the many differences they had. But Sammie's friends clearly rallied round. We were so pleased when she described how they had helped her with the move, then organised a 'moving shower' party at which she was literally showered with gifts to help her establish a home on her own. What kind and thoughtful people. We video-called regularly during this period to make sure she was not regressing mentally, and were pleased to see her adapt quickly to her new life. She was frankly so relieved to be out of that toxic relationship that she quickly overcame any nervousness about living alone. Besides, she was not entirely alone as she had Hugo for company. Time and again we realised that her employment was a genuine lifeline. Sammie had thrown herself into this job and her enthusiasm and determination was paying off. Shortly after moving into her apartment she was given a promotion and asked to help develop the business by opening up an operation in Columbus, the capital city of Ohio. It was a 2-hour drive from Cleveland, and her task was to recruit a network of dog handlers, train them on the job and then find some clients for them to service. It was a real challenge for anyone, let alone a woman in a foreign country who was recently divorced and living on her own. But Sammie took it on wholeheartedly. It wasn't easy to find staff because dog handling is not the most dynamic of jobs, but it carried a degree of responsibility that made the selection of the handlers really important.

Perhaps for the first time in her life, I could see that the personal skills she has could be used to provide a valuable service to her employers, and she realised it too. There were a few false starts with people initially taking on the job before realising it was not right for them and when they signed up the first Columbus client, the dog handler had to be Sammie herself! This meant that she was spending several days a week in Columbus, but once again her amazing friend Roberta was happy to house Hugo but it must have been quite a juggling act initially.

Once again, the roller coaster was running. Everything was going fine, and with a job she loved, and a comfortable and cosy apartment to live in, Sammie's life seemed at last to be moving forward. But then, the next tragedy loomed.

Her step-father David had survived multiple health problems in recent years, including throat cancer which meant that he could only have limited speech. It made communication difficult for their family and especially for Sammie, but she always spoke to David every week and regaled him with stories of her new life in America. We liked David. He was a typical northerner, tough and resilient, and able to deal with anything that life threw at him. This pragmatic approach to life was epitomised by the phrase he often used when confronted with difficult situations, and it is one that I now find myself sometimes using, 'what will be, will be!' We used to see him and Tina once or twice a year when they came down to visit Eve and Sammie, and he and I would talk golf. We even spent several Christmas Days with them both at Eve's house, and were able to put the trauma of my divorce behind us.

Sammie loved David and as she had grown older, came to realise what a steadying influence he had been during her unhappy childhood years before she came to live with Jane and me. So when we heard that he had been rushed to hospital with breathing difficulties, we felt that the signs were ominous. It looked as if his life might be coming to an end, and that once more Sammie would have to face up to yet another emotional crisis. Would she be able to cope, so soon after her own mother's death and then the divorce from Carolyn?

Sammie spoke every day with her sister Eve, who yet again had to shoulder the responsibility of handling the final days of David's life and the subsequent issues that inevitably followed. David died peacefully, incredibly in the same hospital and apparently in the same ward as Tina had passed away. It must have been doubly stressful for poor Eve, who had to be present at David's passing, this time without the physical support of her sister thousands of miles away. They had made the decision that Sammie would fly back for the funeral, and she asked Jane and me if we would come to the service. Naturally we said yes, because we wanted to support both of them at yet another difficult and emotional time for them. Eve was characteristically brilliant, masterminding the practical arrangements with David's two sons. We drove up to the crematorium and after the service we all went for refreshments at David's golf club where we were joined by many of his golfing pals. It was a sad occasion, but the girls got through it and Sammie was able to spend a few days with us before returning to the States. Once again, her employers had been most sensitive and understanding, allowing her to take compassionate leave and stay on to spend time with her family. She returned with a heavy heart, but I think mentally strengthened by the closeness and love we all felt for each other at this difficult time.

Then came the next setback. Hugo had unfortunately had a fall whilst out walking with Roberta. They had to take him to the vet and it was not good news. He had torn a ligament and would have to undergo surgery. By this time, he was getting on in years. Labradors have a relatively short life, and this was the equivalent of an 80-year-old gentleman having a major operation. Once again, the pendulum of fate had swung against our Sammie, and we were faced with the very real possibility of yet another death in her family.

Chapter 13

I'm not superstitious either, but I'll go along with this!

IF BEING SUPERSTITIOUS IS THE last residue of my daughter Sammie's long struggle with clinical depression and anxiety, I'll take it!

Chapter 14

Dealing with Hugo's death. Will she be able to cope?

CHRISTMAS WAS A TIME OF great joy for us because Sammie was able to come home. Meeting her at the airport was exciting, and naturally emotional because we hadn't seen each other since our traumatic time in Cleveland. But she quickly settled in, dividing her time between our home and her sister Eve's.

One thing that particularly pleased me was how the two girls (or should I now say, women!) had become closer since their mother's death and despite Sammie's move to America. Eve had been particularly critical of Sammie's decision to go and live in America with a woman whom, we all felt, she hardly knew, but once the sisters were together, we could see how they had bonded emotionally. They spoke frequently and I expect shared confidences that sisters can do, when perhaps they would not with their parents. Sammie and Eve went to church together to light a candle for their mum, and we managed to get her temporary membership at our health club *Champneys* for a couple of visits. I must admit I never expected to be side by side with my younger daughter on the treadmills! We made the best of Christmas that year for her, and it was truly a happy family time together.

All too soon it was time to say goodbye again. Those moments were never easy for any of us, but we were getting used to it, and at Heathrow we continued our agreement to say goodbye outside the terminal. So, the phone call from Sammie later, explaining that she had been refused access to her flight was unexpected to say the least. I immediately began fearing the worst, that she would never be able to return and would be permanently separated from Hugo. And I think her treatment by USA immigration was unfair and quite out of order. She told us that before leaving she had telephoned them in America to get confirmation that her current documentation would allow her re-entry on her return, and she was assured that this was the case. So why on earth was she barred from flying at Heathrow? It was clearly a case of the left hand not knowing what the right hand was doing. She had to get into central London and join the line for entry into the American embassy, but there again she was refused by the security man because she didn't have an appointment, despite having been told that because she was already living in America this would not be necessary. Left hand and right hand again. And what was worse, she was then charged a big fee to get what they considered was the correct paperwork when the mistake was clearly theirs. Bloody bureaucracy!

I had to go and collect her from Heathrow once she had returned, without the papers but with an appointment a few days later. She was naturally distressed and worried that she might not be able to return. Whilst it was lovely having her with us for an extra four days it was naturally a difficult time, especially for poor Sammie. Well of course she had the embassy appointment, received the papers and was able to fly back to New York, where she was once again subjected to a series of stressful interviews before eventually being allowed back into the country. But this episode actually had a happy ending, when upon arriving at Cleveland there was a surprise welcome committee complete with balloons and happy smiles!

Sammie quickly resumed her normal routine, but then came the moment we had been dreading. Hugo became unwell, and it soon became apparent that it was serious. He had a massive growth and the signs were ominous. Quite frankly, Jane and I were very anxious at the thought of Sammie having to deal with this without our presence and support, and we seriously considered flying out. But we were too late because on the advice of her vet and having seen the scans of the tumour, Sammie had to take the terrible decision to end poor Hugo's life. How do you comfort someone when all your conversation and communication is conducted online? It was hard, and we felt devastated for her. But once again her wonderfully loyal friends stepped in to help. Her boss Marsha and friend Roberta, who looked after Hugo when Sammie was in Columbus, rushed to the vet in order to be with her at the end of Hugo's life. It must have been so traumatic, and back in England we were all so sad and concerned for Sammie's mental well-being. How would she react to his loss? Would it affect her mental state, which for many months now had been so much better? We feared that this could induce another bout of depression, and worried that she would not be able to cope.

But we had reckoned without the new strong Sammie. She now had coping mechanisms designed to help her deal with the crises in her life, and gradually she managed to control her emotions and start to resume her previously happy and fulfilled activity. We know that she will never forget the part played by that lovely dog in helping her to combat her depression. He was for a period back in England literally her lifeline. He was such a special animal and everyone who met him loved him to bits.

It is now some months since Hugo left Sammie, but after an initially difficult period she has come to terms with his death. She has a tattoo on her arm with the word Hugo and she has loads of photos which appear regularly on social media. More importantly, she has survived her latest tragedy and has found the means to move on without regressing into depression. We are extremely proud of her for finding the mental strength to overcome all these setbacks, and are pleased that she has found a way of life that clearly suits her. We miss her all the time but enjoy keeping in touch, and plan to meet up with her as often as we can.

On one of our recent conversations, I suggested that we conduct a question and answer session as a way of completing her story. I wanted to hear from her how she thinks she has coped with everything that life has thrown at her, because there will inevitably be other crises and unhappy moments in the years to come. You know what I mean, I'm sure. So, our final chapter records my questions to her, and details her responses. She also questioned me on how Jane, Eve and I managed to cope with everything in her life so far, and I have answered as honestly as I can. We both sincerely hope that, whilst this is in no way a medical self-help book, her explanation of her coping mechanisms and my comments on the parents' reactions to it all will be of use to others who have had or are still having to face up to the much-misunderstood affliction of anxiety and depression.

The authors in New York, discussing the manuscript.

Richard and Jane.

Chapter 15

One amazing daughter! One incredible recovery.

HAVING JUST READ SAMMIE'S CHAPTER 15 for the first time, I find myself swamped with a mixture of emotions. Surprise, amazement, delight and thankfulness. So, I'm going to write my final response in the form of a personal letter to you from your Dad!

Dearest Sammie,

Looking back over your life as you have recorded it in this book of ours, I can hardly believe that you have arrived at the place you are now in.

One of my earliest memories of you was at my marriage to Jane, when at the first opportunity you discarded the pretty dress and hat that she had chosen for you, and donned your favourite one-piece boiler suit. As I recall from nearly 40 years ago, it was at least pink! It must have been in your genes, because then our little tomboy girl grew into adolescence, discovered that she was gay, and hit a brick wall in her life.

It must have been so hard for you to come to terms with the bullying about your sexuality and the inevitable consequence of not being able to achieve the academic standard that you were obviously capable of, and it was difficult for us to know how to react to your sexuality. In those days, and remember we're talking about over 30 years ago, attitudes were very different and children can be so cruel to each other.

I couldn't wait to get you back to living with Jane and me, and I wish we had talked to your mum earlier because as it transpired, it was not the emotional wrench for her that we had expected it to be. But you arrived and quickly established a new lifestyle for yourself. Except then the emotional tsunami inside you started to build, and none of us could anticipate the awful consequences. At times it seemed that you were falling into a black hole from which you would never return. Try as we might, the force of your depression was just too strong for us to combat, and your life became a misery. As Churchill once described it, the 'black dog' had got hold of you and wouldn't let go'. I vividly remember you even saying once that suicide was your best friend. What a terrible place you were in in those days.

Your attempts at relationships always seemed doomed to failure and we often wondered why, because to us you were just 'our Sammie', a delightful girl and then young woman with a generous nature and no malice at all in you.

Then Hugo came into your life and literally became your lifeline. He helped you through the really bad times, so you were never really alone. And gradually things got better. You made a success of Pets Alone, and we thought that the future was looking brighter. But then you met Carolyn and decided, despite all the family's words of caution, that this was an opportunity for a new start. It was a natural reaction and one which we could understand, but we always believed that it would end in disaster. After having visited you in Cleveland, we knew that the sooner you left that woman the better you would be, but we worried about how you would cope with life on your own again. And when Hugo passed away, we were genuinely scared that you might be dragged back down to the dark days of depression and would feel that you had nothing to live for. How wrong we were.

Moving into your own apartment proved to be the best thing you have done, because it forced you to come to terms with your life and to find your own way to survive. And you have not only survived but are flourishing, which makes us so very happy.

You have said that you do not want to enter into another relationship, but time will tell. Perhaps one day you will find someone you want to spend the rest of your life with, or perhaps you will just continue to be a free spirit enjoying your hard-won independence. The one thing we now know, is that you have become a mature and wise woman who for the first time is in control of her life, and who is loving that. So, whatever it is that has got you to this place, keep doing it!

Just before we finished our story, you announced that you were in a position to buy a home of your own in America. To Jane and me, this is symbolic of the stability you have discovered in your life, and that makes us very happy.

In conclusion, I want you to know that whatever the future holds for you, Jane and I will always be here for you.

Let's finish by conducting a Question and Answer session that might help other people who have been or are going through some of the situations you have so vividly described in our book.

Your ever loving and devoted Dad. X

Chapter 16

SAMMIE'S AND RICHARD'S Q & A

RICHARD:

Sammie, there's no doubt that your life so far has, to put it mildly, been something of a roller coaster. So what made you want to write this book in the first place?

SAMMIE:

It's quite ironic really as I'm not a big reader of books and much prefer the movie versions! I can count on one hand how many books I have read in my lifetime. It isn't through a lack of trying but I simply didn't have the head space and the ability to quieten my mind which was required in order to take in pages of writing. But I believe this came about when I went to see a spiritual medium. Inevitably my mum came through and it was she who suggested writing a book. There was no indication of the subject matter at the time but it was as clear as day what the book should be about. In addition, I am fortunate in that I have overcome years of a debilitating illness and this seems the perfect vessel in which to let people suffering with their own struggles know that there is always hope.

RICHARD:

I think we must concede that there are parts of our book that were pretty tough to write, both for you and for me. Did you have any qualms about committing this story to print?

SAMMIE:

Yes, absolutely. I liken it to a second 'coming out'. There are many parts in this book that my family were not aware of and there are friends of mine who were not aware of any of my experiences, until now.

I knew that a project like this would not be without its challenges and I was right. I also knew that I needed to cover every inch in detail and be prepared to describe my darkest moments.

Here's an interesting point. In order to keep it raw and deeply meaningful I made the decision early on not to read your chapters until the very end. The temptation to protect you from further hurt would perhaps have meant that I wouldn't have been as truthful as I have been.

How about you, Dad, did you have any qualms?

RICHARD:

Well, I must be frank and say that when you first told me that you wanted to write your story, I never thought you would be able to do it. But you did, and I'm really proud of you for that.

I did have a few wobbles during the writing, for example when we first took you to the clinic and had to leave you after lunch. You were so obviously unwell and I wasn't used to that because we have always been a healthy family, and it was a shock to realise that you were in such a very bad place.

I remember when this all started, Jane, Eve and I reacted predictably, which was to try to get you to 'snap out of it', but we quickly learned that you should never say that to someone who is suffering from depression. We now know that it's the worst possible reaction, but it's natural because in the early stages of your illness we simply didn't understand what a grip it had on you. We simply didn't know what to do or say, because no matter how hard we tried, nothing worked. All we could do was to try and support you with love and compassion, and to constantly tell you that our home was a safe place you could come to at any time, but it was tough. Over the years we have learned so much about anxiety and depression, and of course it has now become recognised as a major problem in society, particularly amongst children and young adults.

Now that our book is finished, have you found it in any way helpful or has it been a painful reminder of your roller coaster life?

SAMMIE:

To be honest, I don't need reminders. I am very aware of my actions and my experiences. When I first started writing, there were times when I was quite emotional having to recall the memories in detail. As I got further into the book, I learned to capture the emotion without having the feelings attached. That was something new I learned as a result of this project. In terms of it being helpful… if just one person is inspired by my story then yes, it has been helpful.

RICHARD:

Dear Hugo was such an important part of your life. Everybody loved him so I think he was a very special animal, and we all know just how much he meant to you. Now that he has gone, do you see yourself getting another dog?

SAMMIE:

As far as my own personal dog is concerned, not right now and not in the near future, for three reasons. Firstly, I can't see myself loving another dog as much as I loved Hugo although I am sure that will change. Secondly, I don't know whereabouts in the world I am going to be living for the duration of a dog's life. And thirdly, I want my freedom, to travel and to go out with friends and not to have to come home that same evening.

RICHARD:

Looking back on your life so far and with the benefit of hindsight, is there anything you would have done differently?

SAMMIE:

I'm so glad you asked that. When people go through a life-changing trauma or indeed are born with a disability of some kind, they are often asked, 'would you change what happened to you?' and a typical response is, 'no, it has made me who I am today'.

My response, however, is, 'yes, absolutely, I wish I had never gone through any of it'. But I do wish I had been less resistant to therapy. My years of depression told me I didn't want to be helped and so I wish I had fought harder to overcome that aspect and had accepted the help that was being offered earlier on. I also wish I had spoken about how I was feeling sooner. Maybe then the cycle could have been interrupted and it wouldn't have been so traumatic. I would like to think that with the media coverage of mental health and the stigma breaking down, it is becoming easier to talk about things. I hope this book contributes to that also.

What about you?

RICHARD:

On reflection, I don't think there is much that Jane and I could have done differently over the last 30 or so years. We just tried our best to be good parents in absentia for the first few years of your life, and then to build a strong bond between the three of us when you came to live with us and when you started to live independently. And I'd like to think that we have succeeded in that.

If there is one piece of advice I could offer to anyone in our situation, it is to be constantly vigilant. If you can spot the signs of depression in its earliest stages, it's more likely that you can help the sufferer or seek help quickly from professionals.

We are still conscious of your condition, and are mindful that mental health issues can re-surface at any time. But I am confident that because you also know that, you now have the tools to deal with any issues that may arise.

Reading our book makes me proud that you have overcome so many obstacles that would have left many other people unable to cope. But the overwhelmingly positive point is that living through your years of unhappiness has given you a deep understanding of the complexity of the human condition, but also of the strength of will that you have developed. I firmly believe that you can cope with anything that life throws at you now, but equally that the worst years are behind you and the good times have arrived.

SAMMIE:

Thanks, Dad.

Finally, what would you say to parents, people like you and Jane, who have had to cope with or who are still coping with children or adults suffering from anxiety and depression?

RICHARD:

Wow, that's a big question.

Firstly, I would tell them never to say 'pull yourself together'. Until you were diagnosed, we had no idea just how powerful and destructive the brain can be when it goes wrong. You need sympathy and empathy, but also a feeling that as parents, you are always going to be there for them come what may. Just remind yourself that being a parent is literally a job for life.

Secondly, don't be afraid to seek help. I'm not a professional psychiatrist, but I quickly realised that this was no ordinary illness. It's something that needs specialist help, and fast. But that's the problem. The current inadequate mental health resources of the NHS in the UK have been widely reported, so you must be prepared to go privately if at all possible or be determined to get treatment for your child as soon as possible.

Mental health treatment is not a one size fits all situation because every sufferer is different. CBT will help many patients, but for some it doesn't hit the spot. Equally, we've seen the impact that strong chemical medication can have, and it's not always positive. You are now well enough to know which medication to continue taking and how much, and that will differ from person to person. So, make sure the sufferer is on the right medication for them, and if it isn't working, insist that it is changed.

For most of the time in the clinic you were like a zombie, and that was horrible to see. So I would recommend exploring all options, including complementary alternative therapies such as herbal remedies, yoga, meditation, homeopathy and change of diet before resorting to in-patient treatment.

I also think that exercise is one of the very best forms of anti-depressant, but it's not always easy to persuade a depressed person to do it. Inactivity seems to be a characteristic of depressives, but regular activity is so beneficial that you must persevere.

There is one other thing that is close to my heart which has helped me during difficult times, and that is music. It's interesting to see the explosion of choral singing that has swept this country and perhaps others too. I know that asking people with depression to break into song is perhaps a bit ambitious, but I am convinced that listening to music of all kinds can be highly therapeutic, and so I would strongly recommend it to parents and of course to sufferers too.

I have been struck by a review published in the Literary Review in February 2018, written by Alastair Campbell, of the book *Lost Connections: Uncovering the Real Causes of Depression* by Johann Hari (Bloomsbury). He believes that depression is not caused by imperfections in the brain, to be cured by a pill, but by imperfections in our lives and the way we live them. He castigates modern society for such things as junk food, disconnection from work, childhood traumas, abuse, even disconnection from the natural world. I don't personally agree that medication is a bad thing, and indeed the author concedes that it can work for some people in certain situations. But I heartily endorse his view that many people have become disconnected from the things that really matter, and in today's frenetic society it is so easy to fail to recognise the early symptoms of depression.

I would say to all parents, particularly of teenage children in today's highly pressurised world, keep a watchful eye out for those disconnections because they may just be the early symptoms of something far more sinister.

But above all, NEVER GIVE UP HOPE. Because if you who are well give up, perhaps they who are not well will give up too. As our readers will have realised from reading your story, there is always light at the end of the long tunnel. YOU CAN SURVIVE, and with the help and love of your parents, family and friends, YOU WILL SURVIVE.

By the way, is there anything you wish WE had said or done differently during the years of your clinical depression?

SAMMIE:

That is a difficult question to answer because during the time that I was in the depths of depression I wasn't able to see or feel anything outside of my own brain. I didn't have any concept of how my illness would impact on anyone else including the people who are the closest to me. I was too consumed in myself.

But looking back now, honestly there was nothing more you could have done for me, but perhaps more you could have done for yourselves. As parents of the patient, I realise now that you were also suffering. When it comes to any illness including physical ones, it is useful to have knowledge. But as depression is an illness you cannot see, I think it is even more important for the family to acquire knowledge early on in order to gain a better understanding of the complexities and also to seek support themselves. Being able to speak to people whom you know are experiencing or have experienced similar issues is huge. Every case of clinical depression is different and unique to the sufferer. But they have some common symptoms and to talk to other people who share those similarities would, I am sure, have benefited you.

Again, and I would like to reiterate, there was nothing more you could have done for me, you did everything above and beyond what would have been expected.

RICHARD:

I think that you should have the last word, Sammie. What final advice would you give to people diagnosed with anxiety and depression?

SAMMIE:

Recovery is always possible but it takes time. Falling into depression doesn't happen overnight, it is gradual over many months or sometimes longer. The recovery is the same.

Don't expect to do it alone. Share your thoughts with someone you can trust and don't be afraid to use the words 'depression' and 'suicide', if that is how you are feeling. They are brutal words and naturally we want to protect our loved ones by not using them, but recovery requires you to say them. It's like an addict admitting to their addiction, that's the first step.

Secondly, take help from whichever direction it is coming. That may be in the form of psychiatry, psychology and indeed medication or sometimes a combination of all three. Explore your feelings and make the connection with the emotion, then break it down and dissect it. See if you can answer your own question of 'why am I feeling like this?'

Don't see depression as a weakness. It means you are strong. You are pushing your mind and body beyond the limit it was intended. Just look what happened to me. A realisation at an early stage that I was gay. Unsuccessful relationships, unhappy liaisons, the death of both my mother in England and my step-father whilst I was living in a foreign country, and then losing my beloved best friend Hugo. But…

I HAVE SURVIVED.

Not only that, I can honestly say that I am happier now than I have ever been, despite being a long way from my much-loved family. I have a great job, wonderful friends and a lifestyle that suits my temperament. So in summary, I can now state that at long last, I have finally defeated the black dog of depression.

THE END

SAMANTHA'S POSTSCRIPT

NINE YEARS AFTER MY LAST relapse, I consider myself in full remission from clinical depression. When you hear the word 'remission' it sounds like you should associate it with being free from cancer, but I had clinical depression on and off for three decades and it means that I am vulnerable to it returning, and so I think the word 'remission' is very appropriate.

A lot has happened in the three years since my marriage ended. In my career I have continued to move up within the company. This year is my fifth-year anniversary with them, and I continue to be grateful for my job every day.

After a great many problems during the application process I have also finally received my 10-year Green Card, which means I am able to live and work in the USA indefinitely. At the end of the 10 years I can simply renew my Permanent Residency or in April 2020 I will have been a Permanent Resident for 5 years which will enable me to apply for my citizenship. Fortunately, the UK and USA allow for dual citizenship.

It's the final stage in a very long and often stressful journey. To be a positive representative and a citizen for a country and culture that I love is a gift. It's not a decision I make lightly and there is a lot of emotion involved in it. To achieve United States citizenship will give me a huge sense of accomplishment as well as pride and it is for all of those reasons that I will most likely apply next year.

Just six months ago I bought my first house entirely on my own. A three-bedroom single floor home just a 5-minute walk from Lake Erie. In fact, it is the only street in the town where there is no house overlooking the lake, so I get to see the water every day from my driveway on Sunset Road. I feel incredibly fortunate to have my own home and the biggest compliment I receive from guests visiting is to be told it has a really nice energy. It's a happy house, very quiet for much of the time but there's no feeling of loneliness or emptiness.

I guess the only trace of my mental health is how my home functions. Everything has its place, it's always very clean and all my possessions are exactly where they should be. Everything I own has a function, either practically or emotionally. The rooms are simple with not much on the walls nor an excess of ornaments or furniture and its colour is coordinated throughout. I know I take the organisation of my home to the extreme and while it gives me comfort, I am willing to put some work in to overcome the obsessive need for order. Just this past weekend I was told it was slightly intimidating. I totally understand and acknowledge that, which is why I am prepared to make some changes.

When my marriage ended 3 three years ago, I made the conscious decision not to get romantically involved until I was fully healed. As you know from the previous chapters I like to feel, process and accept every emotion including the negative ones. Of course, three years ago I said to myself, 'I am never having a relationship ever again', but the hard work of getting to a place where I am healed from the break-up has paid off and I am very well equipped for a new relationship. A few months ago I met someone who is kind, thoughtful and caring, which is a refreshing change. Unlike my past relationships I am being cautious. It is early days and I am very aware that the honeymoon period does eventually come to an end. But what is different about this relationship is that I was happy before I met her, and I know that I would be without her. She helps maintain my happiness and gives me experiences where my happiness peaks, but ultimately I will do just fine should this not work out for us.

The key to this is the 3-year break I had. It gave me time to get to know myself again and accomplish things that previously I thought I could only do with a partner in tow. I have a clearer sense of the qualities I look for in a partner now.

I'm not especially materialistic so job, money, car and stuff doesn't matter that much to me. It's the kind-hearted soul that shines from someone and that they want to share with other people that appeals to me.

We are living in a cruel world right now and it is sometimes difficult to see the good that people do. I am guilty of that sometimes, so I like to keep my social circle relatively small. Everyone in my life adds value to me and to everyone they know. They motivate me, inspire me and support me. And I hope to do the same for them. That is what is important to me now.

Because I am in the best psychological shape of my life, I am now ready to be in the best physical shape of my life so I have signed up for a fitness program with a coach. I have lost a considerable amount of weight and I am loving my new lifestyle. When I open my eyes at 5.30am I am no longer faced with dread because I can't stand the waking hours, instead I am content with what my day will bring and at the moment that is the gym at 6am, a walk at 7am and the job I love at 8am.

My social life is in a constant state of immense happiness and satisfaction just like my alone time. With the physical changes I am making to myself it won't be long until I reach the peak of contentment. Something I never knew existed, let alone believed was achievable. That is when I will most likely start a program to come off my medication. It will be slow and very controlled, and I will maintain a great awareness of myself. I do get nervous when I think about it but excited at the thought of it. I see no reason why I can't come off my meds and I'm certainly up for the challenge. Should I have a hint of relapse I will be disappointed but I won't hesitate in getting straight back on them.

Where do I see myself in ten years' time? I will be perfectly happy if I am exactly where I am now. Change is inevitable but I am equipped to make the best of all the changes that will come. I would like to travel, learn about other cultures and continue to make memories with the amazing people in my life.

I am one of the lucky ones, I found a way out and so the greatest gift I can give is to use my experience in any way possible to help people who are stuck in that abyss of anxiety and depression. But I will say again that every minute of every day my mental health is the most important thing to me because without it, I have nothing.

Job done. I defeated depression.

RICHARD'S POSTSCRIPT

IT'S SOME TIME SINCE MY daughter and I finished writing her story, so this is a quick update on events since then.

In addition to learning how to cope with her condition, which as you have read, she has accomplished so successfully, there have been other challenges which she has met with equal fortitude. The saga of her application for a Green Card would fill the pages of another book! The first card was lost by her local post office, so she had to re-apply for another and pay the same fee again. But eventually after a great deal of stress and worry, the visa arrived and she was able to visit us in England without fear of not being allowed re-admission to the States. Once again we were amazed and relieved that this latest setback did not cause a relapse.

With her future in America secured and continuing success in her job, she has recently managed to move out of rented accommodation with the purchase of her first house in a pleasant part of town. So, she has put down roots and has a home of her own for the first time since leaving the UK.

But it is in her character and demeanour that we notice the greatest change. Sammie has developed an innate understanding of her role in the world, even to the extent of advising and assisting others with their emotional problems. It's a bit like the hardened criminal who serves his sentence and then returns to society as a social worker dedicating their life to the service of others.

We are conscious that she may never be fully free of depression, and I must admit that this is always in the back of my mind. As she has so vividly described, it can be an all-encompassing, debilitating condition that makes you unaware of anything or anyone else but yourself. So, to see Sammie now so happy, so content with her life and so giving to others is an incredible joy to my wife and me. We really feel that she can cope with anything that life throws at her. There will be difficult moments in the future that she will have to face but none so difficult as that which she has already experienced and overcome in the past. She is now a strong person, and may yet get to the stage where she is completely free of medication, but if she doesn't feel able to do this, she will still be comfortable in her own skin.

We are now so proud of Sammie and all that she has overcome and achieved in her life. And if her story and my response can give hope to others who have travelled this path, then ***I Defeated Depression*** will have achieved its objective.

CPSIA information can be obtained
at www.ICGtesting.com
Printed in the USA
LVHW021513111119
637002LV00002B/438/P